TABLE OF CONTENTS

P9-CKO-855

Connie Haines at age 21.

AN INTRODUCTION

BY RICHARD GRUDENS

It was the Jazz Age of bathtub gin and the three-mile limit. Crystal radio sets and Victrolas filled living rooms everywhere. Vaudeville prospered. Al Jolson immortalized George Gershwin's great new song "Swanee" at the Wintergarden Theater in New York. Bill "Bogangles" Robinson created his own history tap dancing side-by-side with legendary performers banjo eyes Eddie Cantor and Sophie Tucker, the last of the red-hot mamas, belting out her world-famous torch song "Some of These Days." Ed Wynn, the Ziegfeld Follies' "Perfect Fool," enchanted thousands every night on Broadway's Great White Way. It was the generation of the renowned song writers of Tin Pan Alley: Cole Porter, George Gershwin, Jerome Kern, Harold Arlen and Irving Berlin. Broadway scored heavily with George White's *Scandals* and Earl Carroll's *Vanities* sensational revues. Silent films became interspersed with the live entertainment comedy acts of Gallagher & Shean and Weber & Fields.

And, deep in the heart of Southern America, in Savannah, Georgia, four-year-old Yvonne Marie Ja Mais performed in her first public appearance in the Saucy Baby Show at the Bijou Theater, singing and dancing her little heart out. They literally had to stop the band to convince her to leave the stage.

You, of course, know Yvonne Marie Ja Mais as legendary Big Band song star Connie Haines, Frank Sinatra's first lady singing partner on a string of hits they recorded, including "Let's Get Away from It All" and "Snootie Little Cutie," when they both appeared first with Harry James' big band and Tommy Dorsey's famous starmaker orchestra during the Big Band Era of the 1940s. The two singers performed shoulder-to-shoulder for three memorable years.

This is an honest account of the life of Connie Haines, the petite Southern girl with the magnificent voice who sang with the Big Bands then and sings out to all America today. A song star who communicated her songs to vast audiences during Command Performances before four Presidents, and who has enchanted millions over the radio and on recordings for over 50 years, she is a spirited trouper who fearlessly faced frequent adversity, but, through her steadfast faith in God, turned negative portions of her life into a positive, winning force.

Painstakingly, but joyously, and with much humor, Connie and I worked over each word and every photograph: she from her Florida beach home, and I from my office in the woods of Long Island. Her mother supplied us with a surprise scrapbook of clippings and photographs she had kept for Connie during portions of her tours. We developed a steady work rhythm: she jolting her memory—me with unending queries and a ready Mac word processor. We would begin at a point when she first recalled performing, and end right up to the present. I agreed to confer with those she knew and worked with over the years. So, with a complete understanding of what this unique undertaking required, our literary adventure set sail.

"My first biography was written mostly without me. The author tried to do a good job, but I was always on the run, and he knew little about the music business, being mostly known for writing books about religion and celebrated health figures. The book was an unrealistic account of my life, gathered from scrapbooks and news releases, as well as newspaper articles, although, of course, it did contain many truths."

Today, Connie Haines is a true icon of an age of music that is clearly past. Her remarkable mother, Mildred Clements Ja Mais, whom you will also read about here, turns 101 years old on Valentine's Day 2000 and is still the first person in Connie's heart.

"I just saw her today. She's sharper than friends I have who are in their 70's. She is the only one in the nursing home who readily walks and talks. Her memory, past and present, is fantastic."

In 1997 Connie was the catalyst for my book The Song Stars, enthusiastically encouraging the very idea of the book and personally authoring the foreword in her own hand with her trademark green fountain pen on a yellow ruled pad. That was my first close encounter with her. We've been pen and telephone pals ever since.

In reading this candid biography of Big Band singer Connie Haines, you will get to know her as I have and, therefore, love her as I do. We have all enjoyed her music; now we can turn the pages and enjoy the girl herself.

Richard Grudens
Stony Brook, NY
January 2000

FOREWORD

BY JANE RUSSELL

I'm sure you'll have plenty of time to learn about my friend Connie's fantastic singing career because that's what most people know about her. She has always been a very upbeat positive person who has the guts to face today—no matter what the situation—and looks forward to tomorrow.

Her life has not been easy. I don't know many people who have had to face as many obstacles both physically and emotionally as Connie Haines. If it wasn't for her strong faith in God she could never have made it, but she knew without a doubt in the world that "All things work together for good to those who love the Lord and are called according to his purpose." And called she certainly was.

Jane Russell

Connie, Beryl Davis, Rhonda Fleming and I were all involved in the Hollywood Christian Group and had an absolute ball singing old time spirituals which were the very first to be introduced on pop labels, and we sang them in nightclubs from New York, Chicago, Las Vegas, and all the way to Japan. Many people thought it was shocking and sacrilegious but we knew better. We knew the Lord was pleased when King David danced down the streets of Jerusalem and that his wife Michal was punished for despising him because of it. We were making "A joyful noise to the Lord" and we grabbed hands and prayed with our drummer and piano conductor before every show.

I'm sure you'll enjoy learning more about this honorable, faithful, fun-loving, talented, crystal chandelier loving Southern Belle.

Jane Russell,
Montecito, California
January, 2000

Rhonda Fleming

AFTERWORD

BY RHONDA FLEMING

I think it was 1941 or '42 when I first met my dear friend Connie
Haines. We met at the Hollywood Presbyterian Church. My name in those
days was Marilyn Lane. I was named after the singer-dancer Marilyn
Miller, but the studio said that Marilyn was not a commercial name, so I
changed it. Then Norma Jean came along and the studio gave her my
name, so I became Rhonda Fleming after a long search for an acceptable
name.

We would meet at Henrietta Mears' home in Hollywood. We had
some wonderful talks with her. I always wanted to be a coloratura-sopra-
no who specializes in ornamental trills and runs. But, to my sadness, I
found out I really wasn't a coloratura soprano, I was more like a lyric
soprano, so I really wasn't meant to sing those kinds of songs. Still I did
train very legitimately.

Singing "Do, Lord" with Connie Haines, Jane Russell, and Beryl
Davis was a chore. We were all really show business committed
Christians in the Hollywood Christian Group. We kind of grew up together through the years, and, when the girls needed somebody to sing with
them when Della Russell dropped out to get married and live in Mexico,
I said I could do it for maybe a year, but no longer. They had already
recorded some songs, and now they had to re-do some. They had me in
there, and God, it was awful, because, of course, although I could do it
today, in those days I was very trained — too much, in fact. We were sitting doing "Do, Lord" and they'd say, "Honey, you've got to say *Lawd*."
I tried everything to try to sound like them…I finally got it enough, I
guess, but when I listen to those records now I can hear me doing "Do,
Lord—not "Do, Lawd," Guess I really didn't get it afterall.

Connie, of course, was our little leader. Following along, we all let
her do the leading. We performed in New York, Chicago and a lot of other
places. We'd all sleep together in one room, even though we had a full
suite of rooms. Almost like a college girl sorority, we stayed close together. Jane, I remember very well, was always the last one to wake up to go
and get ready. "Jane, for Pete's sake, get up," we would shout on and on.
Later, we found out she was wearing ear plugs.

Connie—she is very professional—and I wanted so much to belt out
the songs like she did. I wasn't able to because I was singing in a light
opera mode for which I was trained. It was difficult to learn to sing dif-
ferently. She would belt out and it would sound, oh, so strong, I was des-

perate to try to sing like she did. It took a long time. She helped me, I finally got it, as they say, and we all had such a great time. We would sing and sing until they dimmed the lights. We did a lot of top television shows like Milton Berle's, Ed Sullivan's, Red Skelton's, and Bob Hope's.

Connie, with all the physical problems, is still going—she amazes me. Her spirit is still young. Connie is the most unique little dynamo I've ever come across in my life. Talent from head to toe. Every time I have asked her for something I've needed, she has been there. She has performed for me in different charities I have chaired, and she won't ever take a penny. She just comes and does the job. She gets standing ovations every time. There's magic in her. She is, as they say in the trade, multi-talented. She believes God has really given her these talents. In spite of her being knocked down with a lot of problems physically, she gets up there and belts them out. It comes out of her in an incredible way.

We're so grateful to have each other, as the years go on, and we don't get to see each other very often, but we keep in touch by telephone to know we are there for each other. Ours is a treasured friendship: Jane Russell, Beryl Davis, and Connie Haines.

She *is* a Snootie Little Cutie, and I love her.

Rhonda Fleming
December, 1999

ANOTHER WORD
FROM JACK AND ELAINE (LA, LA) LA LANNE.

We have been friends for 100 years, Connie and we.

Once, long ago, I told Connie that I always open my talks about health and fitness singing to a Ervin Drake song called "I Believe," the song Frankie Laine made so popular. It just suits my work.

Connie and I were sitting at the dinner table in my California home with my wife Elaine.

Connie and her friend Jack La Lanne sing, "I Believe."

"It's my song," I claimed.

"No, It's my song," Connie replied.

So we sang the song together, and practiced until we got it down.

Then we sang it together on stage and even recorded it. We sounded pretty good. Of course, she has a more lovelier voice than I.

Connie first met Elaine and I at a church meeting in Hollywood, a long time ago. We've been friends ever since. Elaine and I love her and she loves us. Whenever Connie came back to town to perform, we would always drive to her show and make sure we got together for dinner or lunch. Usually, Jane Russell and Rhonda Fleming would join us, if they could. It's been like that forever.

Now, we just call one another when we can, especially on birthdays, and special holidays.

Connie has certainly had her ups and downs in life, but she beats adversity down with her possessiveness and uplifting attitude. She gives us inspiration and love.

And we return it ten times over.

Jack and Elaine La Lanne
Hollywood, California
December, 1999

The Snootie Little Cutie.

SNOOTIE LITTLE CUTIE

WORDS AND MUSIC BY BOBBY TROUP

She's a Snootie Little Cutie
She's a pert little skirt
She's a knockout and a beauty
And a flirt
Such a dapper little flapper
She's just as cute as a trick,
She's a kissy little missy
A vain little Jane,
She's slick.
She's a classy little lassie,
A keen little queen
And although sometimes she's sassy,
And mean
Just a thing for romance is she
Quirrely little girly she,
She's a knockout, a beauty
A Snootie Little Cutie,
Snootie Little Cutie she.

Barbara and Yvonne Ja Mais, 1930.

Yvonne at five on her way to stardom.

Yvonne at nine.

INITIATION TO FAME AND FORTUNE

SMALL BEGINNINGS

Connie Haines begins her story as she begins each day, with this prayer: **"Father God, I place my hand in Yours today. Here is my life. Show me the way. Speak and sing through me."**

"My mother had encouraged me to dance and sing ever since I was able to walk and speak. At two and three I was joining in family sings at parties and on holidays. Mama entered me in those exciting Charleston contests. I won every single time and soon became the Charleston champion of the State of Florida at the age of five."

Somehow, in those early years, dancing and singing got into little Yvonne Marie Ja Mais's blood, her mother, singing aunts and uncles infusing frequent vocal transfusions. Her mother possessed a three-octave range and could have been a professional singer.

"I used to listen to lady singers on the radio, especially Kate Smith and Mildred Bailey. Mother taught me singing and dancing. She coached me carefully, preparing me for what she hoped would be a *future*. She received immense pleasure from my childhood success, and I loved to perform. Mother was always proud of me—and also very critical—and made me exhibit my talents at every opportunity. I even earned some money which my mother deposited in the bank for me. All those hard-earned dollars were later lost, however, when all the banks folded in the financial crash of 1929. Thoughts of a professional career were eclipsed by that terrible economic event."

FAMILY TALES

Yvonne's father died when she was very young. Known to be a good man, talented, and happy-go-lucky, Dr. Henri Augustus Ja Mais, son of Dr. Augustus Ja Mais, was to succeed his father as the head of a large veterinary hospital he had founded. The Ja Mais family was considered the *creme de la creme* of the aristocracy of Georgian Society.

"How I enjoyed going to the animal hospital to watch them treat the animals. I can still recall the pungent odor of disinfectant and the chirp-

1

Mr. and Mrs. Augustus Ja Mais, circa 1918.

ing of the cuckoo clock that hung above my grandfather's rolled-top desk. The fireplace mantle held little peculiar jars of expired animal embryos. I was endlessly fascinated by the variety of animals they tended. It was exciting to watch horses being inoculated and fed medicine. All the animals seemed very large to me.

"I was about five, and my sister three, when my mother and father decided to move from Savannah to Jacksonville, Florida, where we could be with members of my mother's family. It was decided, somehow, that my father would live separately.

"They were experiencing problems in their marriage, and part of the reason for the move was to help clear the air and afford them both a chance to think over their situation, as there was no such thing as divorce in our family. So, my father rented a room in the American Legion Home and came to get us frequently to spend a day with him. I remember the place vividly. It was on the second floor of a large mansion. The room was also very large- a combined living room and bedroom. And it had a fireplace so great in size that we could stand up inside it. I would ask Daddy if we could have a fire in the fireplace?

"And he replied, 'All right! You girls crumple up these old newspapers and place them under the wood grate.' Then my father walked over to a cabinet and withdrew a bottle and a glass. He poured himself a drink, downing it in one gulp. I remember thinking that if my Nana saw that she would simply die, she being the President of the Women's Christian Temperance League.

2

"'Can I light the match, Daddy?' I asked, 'No, you're too young. I'll do it for you,' he said. We enjoyed the flames and roar of the fire. But Daddy was obviously affected by the liquor and now becoming emotional. He reached in the cabinet and brought out a handgun and, crying aloud, told us he wanted to kill himself with the gun if he could not return home to live with our mother and his girls. He actually held the gun to his head, then to both mine and Barbara's head, while crying hysterically and making us promise to tell our mother of his intention. I'll never forget that scene. It loomed larger as I grew older. "

Yvonne Ja Mais before she became Connie Haines.

Young Yvonne remained very calm throughout this episode while Barbara cried aloud. Yvonne somehow convinced her father to put the gun away. Her very young voice was stern, but calming to her father. "Tell her! Don't forget to tell her!" he cried over and over, "She comes back to me or I will kill you kids, then myself." But Yvonne's voice sobered him as she grasped control of the situation.

"I went to my sister's side and placed my arms around her, and she stopped crying. Sobbing, my father handed me the gun. I took it, got up, put it back in the drawer, my hands as assured and calm as my voice. I could feel God's presence helping me."

3

Although that incident remains vivid in her memory, the subsequent details have long since faded. She does recall informing her mother of the event, so the visits with dad became less and less.

"I had four wonderful uncles. There was Uncle Honey Boy. Would you believe that name? He didn't like his real name, Marion Clements, especially since he performed in show business. He sang and performed in some minstrel shows and had his own local radio show that became pretty popular.

"Then there was sweet old Uncle (John) Bubber, who was more like a big brother. He was Big Bubber for his brothers and became Uncle Bubber to my sister and me. These whimsical nicknames down South are sometimes hard to explain. Within the family my nickname was Sweetie Bunch and my sister's Blue Eyes. Uncle Honey Boy became *Uncle Dad* to me. How I loved them all.

"Uncle Bubber played Santa Claus to us kids after my father died. Had we not all lived together, I am sure we would have suffered financial stress. But, at Christmastime we always received big boxes of presents, beautiful dolls, a tricycle, and similar expensive items that to me represented family love and support. Much of this was Uncle Bubber's doing. As he did not have any children of his own. I guess he sort of adopted us.

"And, there was dear Uncle Alan, who was the youngest. He married Aunt Mollie. He took much time out for me and my sister. He played with us, teased us, took us for walks, bought us those childhood impressive double-dipper ice cream cones. He had such talent. He could sing and dance so well. All my uncles had enough talent to go into show business had they wanted to. But that was frowned on in the South as unacceptable for the good Christian life.

"Every one of my four uncles were dedicated Christians, each in his own individual way. The presence of God was important to me all my childhood and throughout

An early "Cutie". She claps, she dances, she sings.

Connie Haines at seventeen.

my life. Uncle Eddie taught the Gospel of Jesus Christ in an evangelical way in the church, later becoming a Baptist preacher. Once, when I was about eight years old, I found Uncle Eddie one morning still asleep on his knees beside his bed where he had knelt to pray the night before. He too, possessed a beautiful voice and sang in church his entire lifetime."

Yvonne's Uncle Eddie was married to Aunt Margaret who, before her marriage to Eddie, was also her Sunday school teacher. Uncle Honey Boy was married to Aunt Doris, with whom young Yvonne was very close. Although only ten years apart, Doris considered Yvonne as her daughter and was the first to marry one of her uncles and move into the large Southern house of the aristocratic Clements family. Her Uncle Bubber married a lady named Clara, who loved to hear Yvonne sing the ballad *"Vaya Con Dios."*

"All four couples have had beautiful marriages. Their secret? They all shared their love of God and made church the joint center of their lives."

Some said Yvonne closely resembled her grandmother. "We called her *Nana*. She had a strong personality. I guess it's true that I looked like her and acted much like her. I'm more French like Nana and my father's family." This much-loved maternal grandmother was considered by Yvonne as a real mother. "She was a true Southern matriarch. Mother and Nana were very much alike and especially strict with me."

Mother Mildred Ja Mais looked much like her father's English ancestors; slender, tiny, and vivacious. She was the oldest of six children. Despite her outgoing nature, she was inherently shy, but deeply spiritual and always a perfect lady. Actually, her mother's activities were a hobby that mushroomed into a profession. Her family was completely against her participating in any form of show business, otherwise Mildred, herself,may have been a successful professional singer. Besides managing

Connie and her sister Barbara, 1940.

her own daughter's career, she taught the Charleston and ballroom dancing, holding private classes, and produced local school revues from which she retained a portion of the proceeds.

"But her *forté* was teaching choreography and coaching voice. She also taught voice placement, which enhanced the natural voice. She believed that talent was unique and God-given, that it should not be altered, only enhanced."

Yvonne's sister, Barbara, who was two years younger, never really shared her own great soprano voice with others. She was able to take advantage of the time Yvonne later performed in New York to receive professional voice training, studying on and off at the Metropolitan Opera House for over a five year period. But, without the drive and dedication, coupled with a fear of performing in front of an audience, her career was short-lived. Yvonne's family roots on her mother's side reach back to the historic Lewis and Clark expedition (her grandmother's maiden name was Clark) to playwright William Shakespeare, and author Mark Twain (Samuel Clemens), in a direct line according to their family tree. Her French father's side consisted of royalty and clerics in the Catholic Church.

"We had so much love in our family. No matter where I went from my early singing career on, I was always so anxious to get back to my dear family in Jacksonville. Each time I wept when I left them and wept again when I rejoined them. They were my happiness, my joy, my security, and my reservoir of human love. It all grew from them."

JACKSONVILLE MEMOIRS

"I can still envision the splendid home of my Nana. When I was just five years old, we moved from the Savannah mansion of my father's parents to the deep warmth of Jacksonville, Florida. Mother, my sister, Barbara, and I moved in with my many aunts and uncles. Some folks thought they were our brothers and sisters. My aunt Molly was only five years older than I.

"It was during the great depression, but, of course, I was not aware of the negative financial circumstances that beset my family. I recall Nana making me a beautiful smocked chiffon dress with a matching poke bonnet covered with colorful, hand-embroidered roses and endless ribbons that trailed under my chin when I wore it. And, of course, I had to have 'Mary Jane' shoes. They were paid for by my uncles.

7

Connie Haines in Jacksonville, 1937.

"The great house was simply overwhelming. Two imposing stories high with seven huge bedrooms and a sizable Southern verandah running three-quarters round the house, every door was fitted with leaded-glass windows. Inside, a magnificent, curved colonial staircase descended to the center of an immense living room, dominated at the opposite end by an imposing, brick-faced, mantel surrounded fireplace with imposing andirons guarding its stone hearth. High, windowed French doors fitted with vertical cremone style bolt-locks led to a formal dining room. Lace curtains graced every window. In every room hardwood floors were always kept mirror-polished, being mostly covered with both oriental and Persian rugs.

"The master bedroom retained its own fireplace. That was Daddy John and Nana's room. There was such respect and loyalty practiced among the members of our family. I don't recall ever hearing a swear word or raised, angry voices—ever. Throughout our lives, my sister and I have never had an argument.

"Sunday dinner, enjoyed at noon after attending church, was always an important event for our family. The best-tasting Southern fried chicken ever, butter-rich mashed potatoes, butter beans with ham-hocks, black-eyed peas, okra and tomatoes, and miniature biscuits that would melt in

8

your mouth comprised our dinner, capped with Ambrosia fruit-salad. Dessert, created by Nana, often would be a three-layered white cake covered with hot fudge and sliced bananas. Oh, what wonderful memories. Although mother could not cook very well herself, I followed Nana and became a pretty good cook. How I loved life in that wonderful house."

THE CALLING

Their lives now well entrenched in Jacksonville, Florida, Yvonne became a student at the Mattie B. Rutherford Grammar School where she began to imagine herself a serious singer, even though dancing was her specialty. "I always felt that Yvonne Marie Ja Mais would one day be a famous singer."

One day at school Yvonne heard there were tryouts for a local radio program. "Unknown to me, my mother was already in touch with the producer, who was no less than Uncle Ralph Feathers, the Major Bowes of the South, and his was the top radio amateur contest being aired on the NBC Southern Network."

When Yvonne arrived home with the news, her mother was waiting:

"Hurry and change your clothes," she said, "We're going right down to WJAX. Uncle Ralph has already set you for an audition."

"I remember that I could not contain my excitement, jumping up and down, squealing with joy. On the way to the studio, my mother coached me carefully. 'Don't wrinkle your nose. (I wrinkle it to this day!) Don't move around too much. Don't overact.' She reminded me to use my hands and to be sure that the musicians played in the right key. 'You listen,' she said over and over, 'Don't sass me back, either. You've got a lot of things to remember, if you want to get on the Sunday show.'"

Facing the camera and getting ready for a career.

It wasn't long before young Yvonne's income began to supplement her mother's. "At the age of nine I was already dancing and singing for the Rotary and Kiwanis Clubs, the American Legion, and businesses like the Barnett National Bank and the Southern Pacific Railroad. Now my mother had to quit work and go with me to manage my career. My income was able to support us all."

FALLEN TROUPER

Then Yvonne's career almost came to a disastrous end. She had suddenly developed a fever and had difficulty breathing one day during dance instructions. "The doctor later diagnosed my symptoms as rheumatic fever and rheumatic heart. I also had a heart murmur, and the walls of my heart were dangerously thin."

She was ordered to bed.

"I wasn't allowed to raise my head off the pillow. Nana and Daddy John became my nurses around the clock. Mother had to go back to work at the WPA. It was still the Depression years. Nana spoon-fed me and bathed and massaged my body to keep my circulation going. She prayed at my bedside, constantly reading the Bible aloud."

Gradually the attacks lessened. Yvonne began feeling better. Aspirin and bed rest were the only remedies besides the prayers her family administered to her. After almost a year in bed:

"The doctor told mother that I could be carried to the Jacksonville Beach to soak up sun and mix with friends. No walking was permitted. I could now administer my own food. No more spoon feeding and drinking with straws. I remember feeling elated."

Then, in a stroke of bad luck, Yvonne drank water from the same glass as her little friend, contracting scarlet fever.

"Back in my bed, they gave me an antitoxin shot, not realizing I was extremely allergic. My body suddenly swelled, my eyes closing, and I began choking on my own tongue."

LIFE'S VISION—A NEAR-DEATH EXPERIENCE

"Then it happened. My heart stopped beating. I died.

"I found myself floating up, up, up within a beautiful, luminous, shimmering white light. Such warmth, love and security enveloped me.

Then I saw my Lord Jesus in a white, flowing robe with arms outstretched saying to me: *'Follow me—and you will be well.'*

"I cannot describe the depth of love I felt. We were so high above the Earth. When I looked down, it was as if an earthquake had occurred. The Earth opened up and bodies were ascending up to us. Then I found myself looking below at my mother, my Nana, and the doctor. I was hovering high above them. I wondered why they were crying. Then I heard the doctor say, 'If she lives she'll be an invalid the rest of her life.'

"I thought, 'Why didn't they hear what Jesus said to me?' Then I felt my mother and Nana holding me—rocking me—kissing me, their tears tumbling over me. They later explained that the doctor had injected a long needle filled with adrenaline directly into my heart.

"I was alive. I knew I was healed. My strength slowly began to come back. My faith soared. I could move around my bedroom, dress myself, and at last be able to sit down to dinner with my loving family. There was never a meal taken without offering 'Grace.' We took turns leading prayer. That's why I have always cherished the phrase:

'The family that prays together, stays together.'"

A RISING STAR

"Then, I did it! At age ten and a half I was offered a thirteen-week contract to sing with a twenty-piece band. Mother signed it for me right there on the spot. I became NBC's Baby Yvonne Marie, The Little Princess of the Air. But, I had been in bed for eighteen months. Now the twenty steps to the bathroom had to be extended to thirty steps around the room into the hall and back. Then forty—then fifty. No singing on my feet could be allowed."

So she sang, sitting on a piano bench. Life size pictures of Yvonne appeared on the sides of Ward Baking Company trucks, advertising and promoting the radio program. The trucks were seen all over Jacksonville. Foremost Dairies was also a participating sponsor . A great number of gifts, cards, telegrams and letters were sent to the young singer:

"Mother was so busy answering mail and trying to manage my career at the same time." Yvonne was beginning to perform all over the state of Florida. Despite her handicap, the shows went on. Yvonne became a success despite the debilitating setbacks.

Yvonne's entire family faithfully listened to every program, always expressing encouraging words for her performances. "I also sang enthusiastically for local church events and charity affairs. I enjoyed singing for anyone, anytime. I still do. I would write my name on my schoolbooks with a star or sunburst around it, or the image of dazzling lights. I knew one day I would have my name surrounded by lights. I was so sure."

Yvonne told her mother of the great adventures she dreamed of one day when she would became a star. "Now be careful," her mother would warn," people will think you are stuck-up. You know, "she added," you must remember to keep your love of God and place Him first. Then He may grant you the desires of your heart."

Mildred Ja Mais brought her daughter to perform at every amateur show, radio show, and Kiddie Club show possible. Vivacious and outgoing, yet not too aggressive, she always hid in the wings of the theaters unnoticed, young Yvonne always feeling her strength nearby while performing. She believed in her daughter, who knew her mother would always be there.

Mrs. Ja Mais would also try to advance the singing career of her other daughter, Barbara, two years younger than Yvonne, who also possessed a naturally beautiful coloratura soprano voice. She tried adding popular songs and dancing to her repertoire, but for her it didn't seem to be the right thing. Barbara later sang beautifully in operettas for many years.

Now, Yvonne Marie Ja Mais' singing career would bloom. Her mother, believing in her fourteen-year-old daughter's talent and ability, decided to take her to New York to try out for the prestigious and popular "Fred Allen Radio Show."

"Nana had a sister in New York, my great-aunt Helen. She lived on Riverside Drive in a tall brownstone house overlooking the Hudson River. Helen's daughter was Helen Folsom, who appeared with Ethel Merman in the Cole Porter Broadway show *Anything Goes*. We stayed with great aunt Helen, shielded from

Connie appears on Fred Allen's network radio show and wins first place. Roxy theater, June 6, 1935.

12

the coldness of a strange city by the warmth and hospitality extended to us by my wonderful family."

Some family members had reservations, wondering if Yvonne could or should succeed in New York: "She'd have to be one in a million," said her uncle Honey Boy.

"I am that one in a million. I am going to be a star."

Her mother scolded her. "Sh-h, Yvonne, don't talk like that. What will people think of you?"

"I just know it, Mama. God told me so, don't you remember?"

Arrangements were made for them to travel to New York by bus. For a week before the show, Yvonne sang as never before, easily passing the audition.

"On Fred Allen's radio show I sang "Lullaby of Broadway," winning first prize and a two-week contract to appear at New York's famous Roxy Theater." Yvonne was overwhelmed when she received a standing ovation. While in New York, she auditioned for the "Major Bowes Original Amateur Hour," the same show that launched the professional career of Frank Sinatra. Although she passed the audition, Bowes rejected her as not being amateur, ruling her ineligible because he considered Yvonne a professional performer. Invitations came in for appearances on one show after another. Her mother carefully screened each invitation. Would they further or enhance her career? Could she be transported safely? Could she perform while seated? The Roxy Theater management built her a special swing to sing from when the curtains parted.

"I was carried from taxi to dressing room to stage. Nobody realized I was anything but a teenager with an immense voice."

There were some difficult moments for the young singer. Re-curring pain occurred in her heart area, creating an inability to catch her breath. "If it happened when I was performing—and it did on a number of occasions—I would sing with short breaths between phrases. The audience thought it was my 'style' of singing. Between breaths I would remind myself, 'I am singing my way through it—I am in the arms of God.' No room for panic. I remained calm, and the trouble would recede." Yvonne retained all the important winning assets, including self- confidence and the joy of singing.

At the Roxy the audiences loved Yvonne's originality, not realizing that necessity was its mother. A light pain, a few short breaths. But, it all really was fine. But, at Earl Carroll's *Vanities* a short time later, she could sometimes hear the drums pounding out their beat: "It seemed to be out of step with my heart. I did not want to worry mother, so I said nothing. Two stage assistants would carry me up the stairs to the wings. Once, when Milton Berle introduced me as 'the greatest 14-year old singing voice in the history of show business,' my mother motioned him to wait, but Uncle Miltie had to tell the audience that I was ill and could not go on."

Fortunately, it was the last acute attack that Yvonne experienced. "I acquired more control during the attacks and eventually developed a sense of confidence instead of panic. When I did collapse, it was always in the wings, never on stage. I used the control method later, drawing on my confidence in myself through God, and it always worked."

Their return to Jacksonville was triumphant. All the local newspapers ran articles on the young singer's New York success and how she captivated audiences.

"Upon returning home, I again attended Miss Jacobi's Private School, where I had been originally tutored since I was ten years old, hoping to complete high school."

But, life took another quick turn for Yvonne. Invited to sing in a Miami supper club, her mother moved them to Miami. The first month an agent called to report that a famous bandleader had lost his vocalist and asked Yvonne to fill the last week of her contract singing with the band. As *Yvonne Marie* she sang for one week with Charlie Barnet's Big Band as the girl singer.

"One week later, I was asked to sing at the number one supper club in Miami Beach, the elegant Five O'Clock Club, for the winter with Howard Lally's big New York Band. On our closing night I celebrated my sixteenth birthday. The very same evening Howard had asked me to travel to New York to sing with his band and to audition for the prestigious William Morris Talent Agency and M.C.A (Music Corporation of America). "

This was the break that would dramatically alter her life.

Arrangements were established for Yvonne and her mother to stay at Howard Lally's home. "Mother would never let me out of her sight. She accompanied me every single night and sat in the club until each show was over, sometimes beyond two in the morning, then took me straight home."

BIG BANDS, BRIGHT LIGHTS

Once in New York, the pianist in Howard Lally's orchestra rehearsed Yvonne in a practice room in the offices of Paramount Music Publishing in the famed Brill Building, the heart of Tin Pan Alley, for an audition.

During one of the sessions, Larry Shane, Paramount president, sauntered in.

"Yvonne, I want you to audition for a new bandleader."

"When and where?"

"Right here…and now, young lady. This guy is looking for a girl singer. When he arrived here a few minutes ago, he overheard you rehearsing."

Yvonne turned to her accompanist, who nodded, and they agreed to meet a young man named Harry James. This tall and lanky musician was pacing the office when Yvonne came into the room. While she sang "I Can't Give You Anything But Love," James listened intently, then, without a word, abruptly picked up and left before she finished her song, leaving Yvonne's voice trailing and the young girl near tears. He didn't even wave goodbye.

"Who…does…he…think…he…is?" Yvonne was flabbergasted, as was both her pianist and Larry Shane. Furious, Yvonne and her mother left the Brill Building quite upset and puzzled.

"Whoever he is, he's downright rude."

"Don't let it upset you," said her mother on the way back to Riverside Drive. Her mother knew very well about men like Harry James, as she was aware of every bandleader and singer around. But, she had always taught her daughter *respect*—and for her to always remain a lady. Reminding Yvonne not to be upset, but to concentrate on the important audition being held the following day with the William Morris Agency, her mother kept her young, singing protégé calm.

The next day at the apartment the telephone rang.

"Is this Yvonne Marie's mother? "

"Yes. Who is this?"

"Harry James. I'm very sorry I did not have the time to hear your daughter finish her song, but I had to meet my band at the railroad station for a trip to Philadelphia. I had almost forgot about them while I was listening to her sing. That's why I suddenly left. But—I heard enough. She is terrific! How would she like to join our band?"

Checking with Yvonne, "Thanks…yes. When would she start..and where?"

"Tonight."

"Tonight!" She turned to her daughter and repeated everything Harry James had said. "It will be at $ 40.00 a week. The opening is tonight at the Benjamin Franklin Hotel in Philadelphia." James was holding on.

15

"You'll have to take that white taffeta gown," her mother said to Yvonne, and "Yes!" to Harry James.

In an hour Yvonne Marie Antoinette Ja Mais was on her way. Harry James and his manager, Pee Wee Monte, picked her up for the three-hour drive to Philadelphia. Upon arriving she learned her first show was to be on NBC radio that very night. She called her mother to tell her to tune in to WEAF, 660 on the radio dial.

"Yvonne Marie Ja Mais is a fine name, all right," said her new employer on the way to Philly. "But it won't fit on the marquee. There will be no room for my name. Anyway, you don't look like an *Yvonne*—you look more like a *Connie*.'" He looked her over and over—"maybe Connie…Haines—you know, it kinda rhymes with James, "said the young bandleader.

"I thought he said *Ames*, since *Ames* rhymes with *James*. At the intermission I found myself signing autograph books and pieces of paper *Connie Ames*.

"So it was that I would forever from that day forward be known to the world as *Connie Haines*. It sure worked out all right." Yvonne actually liked the sound of her new name, Connie Haines.

Her mother told her that, when someone named Connie Haines was introduced on the radio program instead of her own Yvonne, she thought her daughter had been kidnapped or something even worse and was about to call the police—or even the FBI. Then she heard her daughter's voice.

"Connie who?" her mother gasped with relief. "But, that's not Connie Haines. That's my Yvonne. What is going on there?"

The following morning Harry James, Connie, Pee Wee Monte, and the band headed back to New York. On the way Harry stopped off at a place called the Rustic Cabin in Englewood, New Jersey, to hear a young boy singer Harry had heard on the radio recently. His name was Frank Sinatra.

HARRY JAMES

"I was at the Brooklyn Paramount when I first started, and he was playing at a little place called the Rustic Cabin, and I used to hear him on a local radio show from there when I was coming home, and I didn't know who he was because they didn't say. We needed a vocalist for our new band, so the next day I found out where he was, and I went to talk to him, and he wound up joining the band."

ENTER
THE VOICE

"When we walked in the singer was in the middle of a performance with a group. When he finished he joined us at our table. Frank had just started his career after a successful tour with the "Major Bowes Amateur Hour" and was doing a single at the Rustic Cabin. The Rustic Cabin occasionally carried its show on a radio hook-up. Harry had heard Frank singing one night on one of those remote broadcasts and wanted to hire him as the boy singer for his band.

"My first impression of Frank was that he seemed cocky, but cute, and filled with enormous self-confidence. His voice was totally unconventional, different from any other singers I had heard. He seemed to *talk* through his songs. For him the lyric was the thing. I was really impressed with his ego. He acted as if he was already a successful star. I admired his singing voice and obvious charisma. Being a sheltered Southern teenager, I was initially overwhelmed by his personality and sex appeal coupled with a certain boyish charm."

Immediately, Harry suggested Frank Sinatra alter his name, too. "I sure like your style," Harry said, "but we've got to do something about that name *Sinatra*. How about something like *Frankie Satin*? "Frank stood there for a moment, then looked askance at Harry and said quite abruptly, "You want the voice—you take the name." He turned and, exercising his very healthy ego, walked away. He joined the band the next day, retaining his own name: *Frank Sinatra*.

Connie learned the correct spelling of her designated name *Haines* when she first noticed it high upon the marquée of the Atlantic City Steel Pier some days later. By this time Frank Sinatra and Connie Haines were already singing partners. She was just sixteen.

Frank Sinatra and Connie at the Steel Pier in Atlantic City, 1939.

BIG BAND LIFE ON THE ROAD

Exciting as it was, life as a Big Band singer wasn't always smooth sailing:

"Because Harry James was relatively unknown, our band was not booked into the top spots, and life with the band became a series of one-nighters all over the country. "

Harry James was trying to make a name for himself to keep the band going. He had won first place in *Downbeat's* popularity contest, surpassing the long time favorites Bunny Berigan and Louis Armstrong.

They would ride the bus, perform, get back on the bus, and rest while they traveled to the next engagement. After several nights of sleeping on the bus, it was a great feeling for the youthful singer to check into a stationary hotel, actually hang up her clothes, and wash her hands at will, not just when the bus driver allowed, and to lie across a real bed in a normal sleeping position.

"Frank was a lot of fun on the bus trips. He was always in good spirits. He got along with everybody and really pitched in, always doing his share and more. Once, the band's drummer arrived late, so Harry asked Frank to get behind the drums. The opening theme was no problem for the confident and secure novice. Frank simply picked up the brushes and 'dusted' his way through. But the next number was a jump tune called 'Night Train.' It featured an opening sixteen-bar drum solo. Frank grabbed the sticks and pounded away. Harry was so convulsed with laughter that he had to keep his back to the audience."

The new Harry James Orchestra with vocalists Connie Haines and Frank Sinatra had a long and successful engagement at the Roseland Ballroom and Paramount Theater in New York that summer and some shorter engagements at the Atlantic City Steel Pier and the far away Hotel Sherman in Chicago.

HARRY JAMES

"Frank didn't stay too long (with the band) because we were all starving and his wife was pregnant (with Nancy) and she was going to have that baby any minute and he had a chance to go with Tommy Dorsey for $120.00 a week. He was only making $75.00 with me and not getting paid on time, because we were struggling. Connie Haines had to leave for the same reason. So I gave them my blessing and said if things didn't get better with us (the band) in the next six months to get me a job with Dorsey, too."

Connie, Harry James and Frank Sinatra at Atlantic City Steel Pier, 1939.

Bookings diminished for the Harry James band in 1940. There were often weeks between dance dates, the inroads of competition reducing contract values that had to be agreed upon to land a job for the band. At that time Harry was a very quiet, withdrawn man, refusing to share his problems with others. The financial crunch was too much for the band to survive.

With Frank gone and business uncertain, Harry James let Connie go.

"Harry could not pay my way to the West Coast, so I stayed behind with my mother. Frank was with Tommy Dorsey, and I was out of work." When Harry James arrived in Hollywood to play at Victor Hugo's old restaurant, they drew very few patrons, so Harry folded the band.

"I remember singing at a cute club in New Jersey, not far from where Frank made his start. I remember that spot in particular because it was there I met George Albert 'Bullets' Durgom. A creator of new talent who discovered Jackie Gleason and others, Bullets brought me to Frank Dailey's Meadowbrook in New Jersey on the famous Pompton Turnpike. Mr. Dailey asked me to sing. I chose 'Honeysuckle Rose' and, when I left the stage, I saw Bullets standing nearby with bandleader Tommy Dorsey."

19

Connie sings "Will You Still Be Mine" at Hotel Sherman in Chicago, 1939.

"Hey, gal," said Dorsey, "where did you learn to sing like that? And when can you join my band?"

"I nearly fainted. I told him I only dreamed about such a break. I told him that, when I was fifteen, I heard a recording of 'Song of India' and knew I wanted to sing with his band more than anything in the world."

Connie Haines accepted the fifty-dollar a week job from Tommy Dorsey, although she had an offer from Al Donohue's Society Band for $ 150.00 a week. "The money seemed unimportant. I knew God was guiding all of this and that I was faced with an opportunity far greater than money. I hoped I had made a wise choice."

Connie joined the Dorsey band in April of 1940, during an engagement at the Paramount Theater in New York. Her co-singer on the bandstand was, once again, Frank Sinatra. They were back together as singing partners.

She had placed her future in Bullets Durgom's hands. A non-musician, Bullets was once property manager for the Glenn Miller Band and acquired the nickname *Bullets* as a result of his quick moves around and behind the bandstand. A lifetime friend of Frank Sinatra, Bullets eventually became personal manager to Dick Haymes, Jo Stafford, Merv Griffin, and the Pied Pipers. Besides being Connie's manager, Bullets Durgom became Connie Haines' friend, remaining with her for fifteen years. He became an important figure in her future life.

TOMMY DORSEY-STARMAKER

Tommy Dorsey was one of the premier Big Bands of the era. He had just taken on the Pied Pipers singing group with Jo Stafford. Dorsey records highlighted jukeboxes everywhere with pure honest-to-goodness, exciting recordings. The Dorsey band was big business and growing. The band toured the important ballrooms and theaters.

"When we first joined up with Tommy, Frank would work on the same mike with me. It was one of those diamond-shaped double mikes that provide a warm and mellow sound compared to some of the new ones. However, Frank and I developed a little feud because he teased me unmercifully. I had a Southern belle sense of humor and his was strictly New Jersey tough guy. I tearfully ran off stage many times. He would not even look at me when he sang, but just to the young girls in the audience. So I would pick out a young man or two in the front row and direct to him 'Snootie Little Cutie,' 'Oh, Look At Me Now,' or 'Let's Get Away from It All,' when we were both on stage. These young good-looking service or

Connie and her "traveling dad", Tommy Dorsey.

college men would cheer and applaud, and that would make Frank even more angry at me. Well, he had all the girls screaming for him, didn't he?"

Frank Sinatra was a soft-crooner in those days, and Connie Haines belted out her songs. Frank's voice and range matured with time, of course, as did Connie's. Her range increased to two octaves. She is reminded of this fact when she listens to "What Is This Thing Called Love" or "You're Nobody's Baby, "which were the first recordings produced with Dorsey.

"In those days, the recording equipment did not add anything. Your voice had to carry a recording. You had to *have* it, so to speak. Today, singers can get by with less singing ability by utilizing more electronics. Some recording companies can engineer a voice where very little voice really exists. They splice and re-splice to achieve the sounds they want.

"Tommy really worked with us before we cut a record. We might rehearse all day or all night, especially if we were working up a new arrangement. The band was always well-rehearsed, always clean and crisp.

"And, I received only ten dollars per record; Frank received twenty-five. Period. No royalties. Nothing extra. Even though the record sold millions of copies, and some did, we never received one cent more. The whole time I was with Tommy, that's the way it was. He was taking on us unknown kids and training us. So, there seemed no reason for him to share the royalties. He created a style for us. He had Sy Oliver and Buddy Rich work with us too. Buddy Rich, who was a great drummer, and Sy, who was a great arranger, worked hours on end with both Frank and me, teaching us to phrase properly and teaching us timing when we sang swing tunes. A good drummer can inspire the dullest of bands and make them swing to great arrangements, believe me.

"While with Tommy Dorsey, Frank Sinatra and I resumed our hard work as the band singers. Rehearsals, travel, recordings, one-nighters by bus, and many, many sleepless nights formed our daily life. Believe me, we paid our dues.

"After the eight New York Paramount engagements, we prepared for our first cross-country tour of one-nighters, appearing at all the beautiful ballrooms. On the last show there I literally saved Frank's life. As the huge stage was descending into the pit, a group of teenage girls were screaming and groping for Frank. One reached over and grabbed Frank's tie. We were in the midst of singing the finale 'I'll Never Smile Again' with the Pied Pipers, when I heard Frank choking. I could not believe what I saw. These girls were actually trying to pull Frank over the railing as the stage lowered down. I screamed for help over the mike and reached over to Frank, trying to beat the girls off him and release his tie. By then the ushers were racing over and the musicians were helping as the stage hit the bottom. Frank was finally freed...and okay. But, for awhile it was a very hysterical scene. Those were the days Frank and I began having police escorts even when just crossing the street for a hamburger or cup of coffee."

Connie also relates the story about Frank saving *her* from catching fire during one performance: "Tommy had just introduced me, and I came on the bandstand wearing a beautiful black bouffant tulle net dress. Someone apparently tossed a cigarette down from one of the tier seats. It got caught in my net dress and instantly ignited. Before I knew it, I was enveloped in flames. At the same moment, Frank quickly removed his jacket and threw it over me snuffing out the flames. His efforts threw me

23

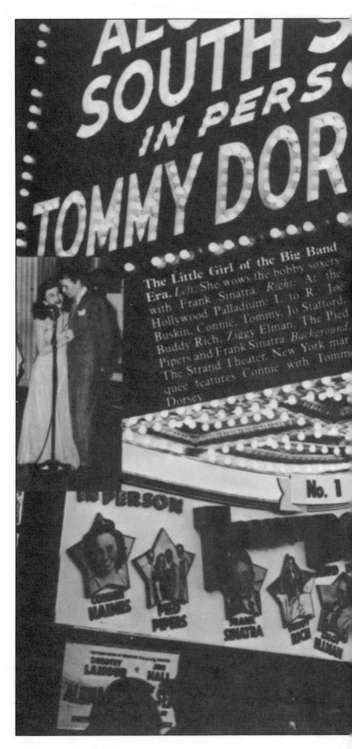

The Little Girl of the Big Band Era. *Left:* She wows the bobby soxers with Frank Sinatra. *Right:* At the Hollywood Palladium; L. to R.: Joe Buskin, Connie, Tommy, Jo Stafford, Buddy Rich, Ziggy Elman, The Pied Pipers and Frank Sinatra. *Background:* The Strand Theater, New York marquee features Connie with Tommy Dorsey.

The Great Tommy
Dorsey Band of
1940.

Tommy, Frank, Connie, Buddy Rich and Tommy Dorsey. Band members Ziggy Elman (trumpet) and Joe Bushkin (piano) in 1940 at Paramount.

to the floor, but my long hair was scorched and the back of my dress was gone. Fortunately I had on a taffeta slip. Unaware, Tommy was still vamping, and the boys in the band looked at each other and Tommy's mouth dropped open when they saw my backless dress with its sides flying. I finished my song with a little more than the usual shake in my voice and backed carefully off stage."

Connie Haines received great revues while with Tommy Dorsey. Damon Runyon, Broadway's elite veteran columnist, described her as "perhaps the only singer now before the public who so enunciates the words of a lyric that a listener knows what they are." *The Washington Post* said; The sultry voice of Connie Haines induced those moments of calm when it turned swing into something sweet—and that sweet is something called *rhythm.*

"I was a stylist. It was more important to be a stylist than to have a great big voice. The orchestras and recordmakers were searching for that individual, characteristic sound. The new equipment in those days could not support a big voice. I had to calm down—pull back. This gave me a 'style.' It was quite different from the way I sing today. I sang then like a drummer, with a beat in my voice. I was said to 'swing.' "Musicians said Connie was both a rhythm section and a brass section rolled into one instrument—her voice.

The RCA Victor tour, called the Dance Caravan, covered eight cities in the Midwest, including Cleveland and Columbus, Ohio. They continued on to Detroit, Michigan, where they played the Michigan State Fair and a few smaller cities. Then the great band of Tommy Dorsey, his musicians, singers, and arrangers, headed for the city of their dreams—Hollywood.

"After months of traveling, we all wound up in Hollywood for the exciting opening of the now famous Hollywood Palladium."

Connie was only seventeen, requiring Tommy Dorsey to appear before a judge to be appointed legal guardian in order for her to leave New York State in order to travel with the band. Her mother was greatly concerned, but realized it was the only way her young daughter's career could move forward.

"By the time we hit California, my mother had packed up Nana and my sister, Barbara, and moved into a little house near the Palladium. They were waiting for me with open arms. I believe I could not have made it—this gypsy life—without the support of my loving family. It kept normalcy and balance in my life."

The grand opening of the Hollywood Palladium on October 30, 1940, was more like a Hollywood movie premier. Huge arc lights beamed into the night, flashing and reflecting over the festive landscape as flashy Hollywood luminaries arrived in chauffeured limousines—Lana Turner, Judy Garland, Dorothy Lamour, Clark Gable, Jackie Cooper, Bob Hope, and many more. Bing Crosby and Bob Hope's favorite sarong girl, Dorothy Lamour, cut the large opening satin ribbon that, together with a pillow of orchids, held the center curtains together. As the curtains parted for the very first performance, Tommy Dorsey performed his beautifully smooth theme "I'm Getting Sentimental Over You" to a standing ovation.

"This was one of the most exciting moments of my life. As I was caught up in this make-believe world, which for now was my real world, I heard the strains of a familiar entrance, one of my own songs, as Dorsey presented me to this enthusiastic audience of five-thousand celebrities, service men, and individuals lucky enough to obtain entrance to this grandiose opening. What a night it was! "

Some of Dorsey's song selections were "Let's Get Away from It All," "Oh, Look At Me Now," "I'll Never Smile Again," "Snootie Little Cutie," "Comes Love," Nothing Can Be Done," "All or Nothing At All," "What Is This Thing Called Love," "Will You Still Be Mine," "Marie," "Song of India," and "Two O'Clock Jump." All those wonderful chestnuts from Tommy Dorsey; the voices of Frank Sinatra, Jo Stafford and the Pied Pipers, as well as the crisp clarinet of Johnny Mince; the exciting drums of Buddy Rich; the sweet piano of Joe Bushkin, and the masterful trumpet of Ziggy Elman glittered like stars in the firmament—ever so brightly.

"What music we made that night in Hollywood! Lovely Jo Stafford became a big sister to me, and Ziggy, well, he was my big brother.

"And what publicity we had for months before our opening. The P.R. guys dreamed up a romance between actor Robert Stack and myself. So, during the first intermission, Robert Stack showed up to introduce himself to me, saying, 'Connie, if we are supposed to be engaged to get married, I think it's about time we met.' Oh, he was so handsome, and had just completed a movie in which he gave singer Deanna Durbin her very first screen kiss.

"I thought to my very young self, 'Could he be the one for me?' But, I was too shy. Bob Stack and I enjoyed a good laugh and hit it off immediately, but just as friends. We never dated. It was strictly a publicity stunt. He visited me during performances at the Palladium, but our get- togethers were merely business. I stretched my imagination, dreaming about seeing myself as his fiancee."

Connie celebrates her 21st birthday with Lana Turner, Jackie Cooper and Tommy Dorsey.

LIFE IN HOLLYWOOD

While performing at the Hollywood Palladium, Tommy Dorsey announced that contracts had been signed for the band to appear in the Metro-Goldwyn-Mayer film *Ship Ahoy*, starring dancer Eleanor Powell.

"I was thrilled. This was our second movie. I didn't receive much of a part—I dreamed of MGM making me a *bona fide* movie star. I enjoyed all sorts of dreams, as a young girl will, but again, I was, after all, just a girl singer with the band."

Getting up early in the morning at 5 a.m. to arrive on a movie set by 7 a.m. was a new experience for a band singer accustomed to performing late night gigs. "It cut sharply into my very limited private life. Motion picture actor Jackie Cooper and I were just beginning to date. He was so cute and I had such a crush. It was difficult enough getting to go out together while I was performing nights and he was making films by day, but this new deal put a real damper on our time. Jackie was living with his mom and I with mine. He was also real close to his mom as I was with mine. He came up every night to hear the band, and we would meet afterwards.

"One night Tommy told us we had to remain late for a special rehearsal. It was my birthday and Jackie and I were planning an evening out. Tommy saw the expression on my face, but turned away. That night, after the show, I received a dozen roses with a card in my dressing room: 'Happy Birthday, Honey, I hope you're as happy as you've made me.' What would I say? He will be so disappointed. I remember wanting to cry. Then I realized the dressing rooms were unusually quiet and no one seemed to be around, so I wandered over to the stage area to check what was going on.

"As I arrived, Tommy's baton suddenly waved, and the band broke out with a loud and cheerful rendition of 'Happy Birthday.' I was totally stunned. The 'rehearsal' was just a ploy to insure I was to be there for this party. I was totally surprised, and Jackie was there smiling among all my friends. Looking back I recall Gloria De Haven, Judy Garland, Frank Sinatra, Lana Turner, Susan Haywood, David Rose, and even mother, all being there to celebrate. It was January 20, 1942, my twenty-first birthday, that wonderful kind of day, and night, one doesn't ever forget."

Jackie Cooper and Connie Haines remained a Hollywood item for a while, as Jackie would follow the band. The couple enjoyed their youthful romance. Tommy permitted Jackie to play Buddy Rich's drums (Buddy and Jackie were friends) during many dances. But, the romance began to fade under the strain of separations due to traveling, the business

New Year's Eve with Tommy Dorsey's Orchestra, 1942. (L. to R.) Tommy Dorsey, Jo Stafford, Buddy Rich, Connie and other band members.

In the Paramount film "Las Vegas Nights" with Tommy Dorsey and his Orchestra, 1941.

of the band, Jackie's own distractions as a contract movie star, and the fact that her mother wanted to break it up. Connie still has the ankle bracelet given to her by Jackie Cooper during that surprise birthday party.

Making a movie, despite the long hours and very hard work,was an enjoyable experience for the young singer. "I had always been an avid moviegoer. As a kid, there were many times when I watched two double features in a single afternoon. Lana Turner, who was now my friend, Jeanette McDonald and Nelson Eddy, as well as Jimmy Stewart and Clark Gable were among my favorites. Imagining myself as a movie star was hard to believe, but we all could not wait until we saw ourselves on the movie screen in a theater."

During the run of the movie Connie recorded Cole Porter's great standard "What Is This Thing Called Love." Sy Oliver had arranged this haunting ballad into a swing version for Connie's clear, crisp voice and Tommy Dorsey's smooth trombone, enhanced by Buddy Rich's drums and Ziggy Elman's trumpet. Connie, to this day, still opens each show with that very arrangement.

However, playing club dates, making movies, cutting records, and appearing at myriad military installations all began to wear on the body that was Connie Haines'.

"One day on the movie set, I felt very headachy. I said nothing. Of course, my mother sensed there was something wrong, but I succeeded in pacifying her. The headaches became severe. I began to shake. I had never been a nervous person. It was, no doubt, a migraine. By the time the picture was finished, so was I."

Tommy Dorsey became quite concerned when the young singer took to her bed. "I'm just overtired, Tommy. I'll be all right in a few days," I told him. "But I wasn't. I had too much pain to rejoin the band at the first uncut showing of *Ship Ahoy* takes. I was so disappointed."

"You were great, Connie," Jackie Cooper reported, peering over the largest bouquet of mums she ever saw.

"Jackie and my friend Lana Turner visited just about every day. The gift of Tuvache's Jungle Gardenia Lana brought me from Paris remains one of my favorite perfumes even today."

Connie remained in bed, sleeping much and eating little. The band headed east without their song star, owing to schedules and commitments that could not be broken. Connie had decided to remain behind in Hollywood to accept an offer by NBC radio to appear in her own show "Here Comes Connie." Her piano player was Skitch Henderson, currently legendary conductor of the New York Pops Philharmonic Orchestra. Tommy Dorsey graciously released the young singer from her contract.

"You know the Frank Sinatra story. Frank and MCA had to buy Tommy out before he would release Frank. Now, you can understand how I really loved Tommy. He was truly a father image for me, treating me as he would a daughter."

Connie settled down. Here she was, a twenty-one year old burnt out kid who never had the opportunity to fall in love or meet other kids her age or to develop meaningful relationships, "I was never able to date much. At a band stop I might meet a young man after the dance, but then I soon had to get on the band bus, frequently to the teasing, embarrassing voices of the musicians calling out, 'Connie's got a boyfriend!'"

On the cover of *Parade Magazine*, photographed in Pottstown, Pennsylvania at the Sunnybrook Ballroom, the photo story angled on Connie's arrival at the railroad station, checking into the hotel, accepting a date on the phone, walking with a young man in the local park, introducing him to Tommy, the show, jitterbugging later, then the good-bye and boarding the train to leave. Later, a surprised Connie was embarrassed when the story depicted her as the girl who sang with the band with a *boyfriend* in every port.

Connie Haines was a spiritual person who needed a spiritual center.

Connie receives USO award in Hollywood, 1942.

In Hollywood she discovered the Hollywood Presbyterian Church pastored by Dr.Louis Evans and teacher Henrietta Mears. It became her church home. She soon became president of the Christian Endeavor Group, which had a sizable youth group.

Signed for a half-hour radio show, singing star Connie was backed by an all-girl orchestra. It was called "Your Blind Date," and was built around participation not only by the military audience in the studio, but listeners as well. Here's how it worked: The show aired at 7:30 P.M. each week from Studio B of Hollywood's Radio City. No civilians were admitted, only 400 servicemen. Besides the music, patter, and comedy, one lucky mother was selected each week to read her letter to her son stationed overseas. Distant sons could hear the program by shortwave over San Francisco's KGEL. Many tears flowed, and, after the show, part of the stage crew from the NBC staff and the USO became the blind dates, limited to dancing in the studio with a jukebox providing the music, including Connie's recordings with Tommy Dorsey, lasting until almost midnight.

With Bing Crosby, Phil Silvers and Betty Grable on radio's "Kraft Music Hall."

In 1943 the Strand Theater proclaims three big names in their first starring engagements: Carmen Cavallero, Perry Como and Connie Haines

"These were men facing the unknown. They were soon off to fight a war. Behind them was their former life—comfortable memories of family, job, and their loves. Only one element of the past remained in the present and would be with them in the near future. Whenever I could, I tried to remind them of their spiritual ties. After each show, I would bestow to each serviceman a small version of the New Testament. It wasn't always easy to do in that setting. Somehow I felt I was in a 'church' when I was with those boys.

Belief in God did not always require stained-glassed windows or a pulpit."

Letters and postcards poured into the studio from near and far confirming the show's success. One letter read: "Dear Connie, received your glamorous photo today. Showed it to the fellows. Don't be surprised if the 7th Squad goes AWOL in Hollywood. After the war, if you ever appear in my home town, Boston, I will acknowledge your photo in person."

The show was known as Hollywood's version of New York's "Stage Door Canteen." One show had over eight hundred air cadets' requests for tickets, so lots were drawn for them. The winners rolled up to the Vine Street parking lot in sixteen trucks.

The show's popularity brought other radio offers for the young singer. She signed a Capitol recording contract as well as a deal to make movies for Universal, and she began live guest appearances on other radio shows. Her former boss, Tommy Dorsey, kept in touch, reassured that his 'daughter' was well, busy, and hoping to return to sing with his band some day soon.

Connie's career began picking up: "I appeared with orchestra leader and arranger Gordon Jenkins at Hollywood's Casino Gardens. Gordy's arrangements enhanced a song and made a singer grateful. 'He Wears a Pair of Silver Wings' was my first hit recorded for Capitol Records."

That recording, which had first been introduced by Dinah Shore, followed by Broadway's Mary Martin (on Bing Crosby's "Kraft Music Hall" radio show), became a hit for Connie. She found her eyes staring back at her from the cover of the show business weeklies *Variety*, *Billboard*, *Radio Life Weekly*, *Downbeat*, and *Life* magazines. "Even what I wore became the subject of a magazine article. I completely altered my hairdo every week on the radio show. One week a vertical row of white bows down the back, another week it was red bows forming a 'v' followed later by a comb with colored ornaments. The May Company, a large department store, invited me to appear as an advisor to teenagers. Life was so exciting for me."

By June of 1942 she garnered a singing spot on conductor, composer Meredith Willson's radio show (who later wrote *The Music Man*), a summer replacement for the popular "Fibber Magee and Molly" show.

Connie never became a negative subject of the tabloids. Her diminished social life was contrary to the fast pace the image-makers encouraged. She shunned the late- night spots unless she was actually performing. But the columnists, just as they do today, invented items, placing her where she wasn't and with people she had never met. All the publicity and exposure intensified, landing her the coveted vocalist spot on the *Abbott*

& Costello Radio Show. Those two comedians had attained great fame, first in burlesque, then in vaudeville and later in motion pictures in the late 1930s. What a break!

ABBOTT & COSTELLO

"It was the season's top show, and I was its singing star. Bud and Lou had wanted to do something for servicemen, so they arranged for the show to be broadcast from an NBC donated stage, forming a large military reception center. After the show aired, we all went to town in an afterpiece for our young military audience. So I found myself again boosting morale for our young men in the service of their country, men soon heading for war zones."

Abbott & Costello were the hottest comics in the country. The radio show was a smash. Connie was in awe, totally thrilled to sing on their show. "Besides a feature singing spot, speaking parts were written in the scripts for me. The thirteen week contract was extended to four years. At Universal (Studios) the three of us made a number of movies. I no longer resented getting up at 5 A.M. It was easy. Makeup people prepared your hair while you enjoyed breakfast on the set. Perc Westmore was my personal make-up artist. Each successive summer we played theaters across the country. While traveling with Abbott & Costello and an eighteen piece band on the Super Chief, the boys carried on a jam session every night in the club car. I joyfully sang my way from California all the way to New York, with many stops in-between."

Lou Costello and Bud Abbott played high-stakes poker each night with pots reaching into the thousands, rivaling Las Vegas poker tables. Connie recalled that Bud would win going—and Lou would win coming back—so they seemed to have evened it out, remaining friends. On movie sets, gambling took place in trailers with many of their gambling friends coming and going all day between camera takes.

"The public never knew that Lou was the businessman, handling all details of their partnership. Bud was the quiet one. Lou was the leader, although you would've thought it was the reverse. They never fought with one another and supported me all the way in my career.

"How I loved those boys. They were like part of my family. I remember a tragic moment in Lou's life. At his home, during a tea party around the pool, his baby boy drowned in the pool when he somehow broke away from his nurse. It was a grievous tragedy. Our radio show was to be that afternoon and Lou still did the show. He said,'I cannot let them (the radio

Connie with Bud Abbott and Lou Costello.

audience) down; they are waiting to laugh.' I'll never forget his swollen eyes and puffed face, but he was never so comical. When the show was over, he broke down, collapsed, and we fell into each other's arms and sobbed and sobbed."

Connie appeared in the servicemen oriented film *Stage Door Canteen*. The vibrato of her inspiring voice and the radiation of her enthusiasm was used as an expression of the country's faith in its military men. She volunteered whenever the opportunity arose. Two nights a week she served at the Hollywood Canteen, dancing one night, singing the next. Film star Bette Davis served side-by-side with Connie and the other volunteers. Every available movie star in Hollywood donated their services.

One day each week Connie visited a California military camp or hospital to sing for the men. The War Department employed her to cut some recordings for the men to listen to while they served overseas.

Connie entertains servicemen in the Hollywood Canteen, 1943.

"I felt then that my calling was beginning to be confirmed. I asked to be used spiritually in bigger and better ways. In January of 1943, the "Abbott & Costello" show went to New York for four weeks and I went with them. It was reunion time. The visit was well-publicized and we were greeted by a battery of cameras when the Santa Fe Super Chief train arrived in Chicago. In New York it was the same. It was great seeing old friends in New York and visiting familiar haunts that had played an important part of my band vocalist days.

"A weekly radio show allows you less time than you would think, rehearsals being what they are. Lou was a disciplinarian. Making movies and performing at personal appearances related to the show, I was unable to attend church and that frustrated me.

"I knew my commitment to God was behind many of the wonderful things that were now happening in my life. I kept re-dedicating my talent to singing His praise. I thanked Him for putting me in touch with the beautiful people I was working with, for the chance to help the men who were on their way overseas to face a war, and for the greater work that He was preparing for me. I knew God had great plans for my life that lay ahead. "

Connie's Nana read the Bible with her, giving her the reinforcement she seemed always to need in those times, and, although tempted to return to Florida to be with her own four sons, stayed on with Connie, her sister Barbara, and her mother. Connie reflected about her dependence on her mother and grandmother. Sometimes frightened of what she had begun, her mother gazed upon her daughter saying, "Maybe show business—is not for you, Connie." But how could she stop now?

"I felt a responsibility to my family. It was a natural thing for me to make sure they were cared for. I loved them so much I never, ever thought otherwise. With no other means of support, my mother and Nana were frequently ill, and my sister, Barbara, was still in high school."

Even then, Connie perceived the spiritual side of people just as she does today. "The public has canonized stars like Marilyn Monroe, Clark Gable, Rudolph Valentino, and Jean Harlow. I saw God expressing love through all these entertainment people."

That February, Lou Costello became ill with rheumatic fever, placing the entire radio team on hiatus.

"In show business it's hard to put down roots. Radio shows usually have summer-time off, and so, in June I was on the road again to fulfill some lucrative offers from major theater operators."

One morning, several months later, Lou Costello called Connie: "Hey, half-pint, how's it going?" He sounded like his old self.

"Fine, five by five, you sound just great," Connie replied. She is just four feet eleven inches.

"Well, what's left of me is good...I lost fifty pounds, Sweetheart. How about lunch with Bud and me at the Brown Derby restaurant today? We'll feast on celery and cottage cheese."

The Brown Derby was a highly celebrated restaurant with telephones in every booth and walls adorned with autographed movie star photos.

"Lou Costello remained a serious businessman, still naturally funny, and never in need of gag writers. Lunch with those guys meant lots of laughs. Lou would clown with the waiter and the people at the adjoining table, but, when we talked business, he was dead serious. Bud usually remained quiet."

They worked out a new contract with Connie, and in a few days they were all back on tour performing vaudeville to audiences across the country and back again to Hollywood. Connie was captivated by Lou's energy. Even as young as she was, she could see this very special chemistry. For Connie, just watching Abbott & Costello perform was a study in greatness.

CONNIE ON TOUR WITH
THE ABBOTT & COSTELLO SHOW
Highlights and Reviews: 1945-1948

The radio show tour began on June 27, 1945 at the Hinchliffe Stadium in Paterson, New Jersey, Lou Costello's home town. It was a tremendous success. From there they appeared for two weeks in New York City at the Roxy Theater. Connie offered deluxe renditions of "No Can Do," "Autumn Serenade"and "I Don't Care Who Knows It."

"Lou Costello and his radio troupe, that includes the delectable singing star Connie Haines, who warbled beautifully for the appreciative crowd, put on a great show," according to the *Paterson Evening News*.

The show traveled to Mechanicsburg, Pennsylvania, but not before Connie appeared at Yankee Stadium with Betty Grable, where the Army Ground Forces staged "Here's Your Infantry," to honor servicemen. Other guests were Broadway actress Helen Hayes, comediennes Lucille Ball and Judy Canova, songwriter Hoagy Carmichael of "Stardust" fame, and actor Dennis Morgan.

The show toured many cities and played at many theaters: Baltimore, Maryland, at the Hippodrome; Hartford, Connecticut, at the State Theater; Newark, New Jersey, with Connie Haines as the highlight of the show and Jackie Gleason as an "extra added attraction," at the Adams

Theater. "Top honors go to Connie Haines when she sings 'My Dreams Are Getting Better All the Time' and 'Pages in a Book' at the Adams and Jackie Gleason who chucks in the gags with clowning and impersonations," said the reviews.

In New York, Connie appeared at the Martinique Club on West 57th Street, at the famous Ciro's and the fabulous show-place-restaurant Copacabana, and even found time to slip in an appearance with Stan Kenton on his popular radio show. Connie has graced the cover of *TV Image*, *Song Parade Magazine*, *Radio Mirror*, *Radio Life*, and dozens of other entertainment magazines, as well as appearing on the cover of dozens of song sheets.

Connie was always the toast of Broadway and Hollywood. Famed columnist Lee Mortimer, in his "Nightlife column," extolled her as the "personable and lovely-voiced Connie Haines, of the radio and stage."

In Earl Wilson's column, "It Happened Last Night,"he noted that "Universal Studios urged Connie Haines to take diction lessons and get rid of her Southern accent, but she said 'No!' Good girl, Connie."

In the" Broadway" column of Dorothy Kilgallen: "pint-sized Connie Haines is in town (NYC) to wed one of the Wesson Brothers?" "No way," said Connie.

The 1947 "Broadway" column of Danton Walker report-ed: "Connie Haines, the 'California Sunbeam' (from Jacksonville, Fla.) will be teamed with Mickey Rooney, both for radio and pictures...to replace an ailing Judy Garland."

Nick Kenny's famous column "Nick Kenny Speaking" reported: "Connie Haines is being feted (honored) at Leon & Eddie's tonight, a well-deserved party, indeed!"

The *New York Enquirer* reports: "Abbott & Costello in rare form at the Roxy. Helping them along is the scintillating and delightful earful, Connie Haines."

The *New York Daily News* said: "Connie Haines, the four feet, eleven inch singer heard Thursdays on the Abbott & Costello NBC series, has been voted by a Marine Corps tor-pedo-plane bombing squadron in the Central Pacific its 'Miss Turret Girl of 1945.'"

a SONG PARADE

LYRICS BY PERMISSION OF COPYRIGHT OWNERS

Latest Hit Songs
RADIO · SCREEN · STAGE

JULY 10¢ 12¢ IN CANADA

ANG

**FEATURING THE
JEROME KERN HIT**

"IN LOVE IN VAIN"

CONNIE HAINES

SONGS FROM BROADWAY HIT

"ST. LOUIS WOMAN"

FEATURING MUSICAL REVUE "THREE TO MAKE READY"

FREDDIE RICH
AND
CONNIE HAINES

Whenever you hear Abbott and Costello on NBC, you hear the rich music from Freddie Rich's orchestra who have accompanied the comedy team on the airshow since their inception. Freddie Rich's orchestra will bring the musical background for the great Hollywood Bowl benefit bill for the Examiner's War Wounded Fund.

Connie Haines, popular and petite singing star of screen, radio and records, recently completed a featured part in the musical, "A WAVE, a WAC and a Marine," produced by Edward Sherman and Lou Costello, which will be released in July.

She first won national fame as singing soloist with Tommy Dorsey's orchestra, sharing vocal honors with the now famous Frank Sinatra.

Miss Haines is now the singing star of the popular comedy airshow of Abbott and Costello, marking her third year on the program.

BROADWAY BRIEFS

Joseph Macaulay is en route to the West Coast for a role in Edwin Lester's production of "The Fortune Teller" for the Los Angeles and San Francisco Light Opera Association "Song of Norway," at the Broadway Theatre, gave its 750th performance the other night . . . After theater crowds are gathering in Topsy's Chicken Roost, Broadway near 48th St.

Josephine Hull has not missed a performance of "Harvey" since opening night. So she takes a vacation, June 10th . . . Beatrice Pearson and Alan Baxter have the leads in "The Voice of the Turtle" . . . Vic Perry, night club vaude entertainer, has formed "Transatlantico Society," an exchange service for actors, which will guide newly-arrived members . . . Buddy Reid now managing Mickey Vitale's new band . . . George A. Putnam now heard in Paramount News Reels.

The American Negro Theatre's production of Frank Gabrielson's "Days of Our Youth," a musical set to book by Kenneth Webb and Joan Alison, and music and lyrics by Maria Grever and Stanley Adams, will be presented next season by Milton Rubin . . . Ed Haywood off to Hollywood for films and club appearances . . . Connie Haines no doubt between appearances.

The Fleetwood Restaurant, open, after being closed for several weeks because of a fire . . . Dining at Allan's Steak Heaven, Lexington Ave. and 52nd St; Ray Bolger, Walter Huston, John Wildberg, Beatrice Kay, Macray Dale, Kate Smith . . . Bob Olin is doing a turn about his ring days . . . Lou Del Carlo in erstwhile Cugat singer, debuting at La Conga with his new band . . . Dining in Kellogg's . . . Don De Leo.

CONNIE HAINES JOINS SHOW

Singing Star of Abbott, Costello Program in Sheriff's Fete

Connie Haines, singing star of the Abbott and Costello radio show, is the latest addition to the Sheriff's Annual Show which is being produced and directed this year by Abbott and Costello and Eddie Sherman at the Shrine Auditorium from October 4 to 11, inclusive.

Miss Haines makes her movie debut in Biltmore Productions' "A Wave, a WAC and a Marine." Her name joins such illustrious company as Abbott and Costello, who will be making their first appearance before West Coast footlights; Jack Carson, Virginia O'Brien, Arthur Treacher, Dale Evans, Belle Baker, Basil (Prof.) Lamberti and Freddie Rich and his orchestra. Fourteen outstanding variety acts nightly will supplement the appearance of these and other top stars.

SINGER—Connie Haines, singer on the Abbott and Costello radio program, who will perform at the Sheriff's annual show.

Joe Clayton and Bob Lerner, back from their honeymoon, were at the Stork. She leaves for Hollywood next week . . . Capt. Fred Barbier and bride, June Exley, ex-Copa dancer, expect a baby in November . . . NBC has banned "22 like a Time, the Corner," claiming the lyrics are suggestive . . . The 400 Club now has a Cement Mixer Cocktail, "one drink and you're plastered." . . . Joey Adams, at La Martinique, noticed Connie Haines' new coiffure, "Your hair's dirty," he said, "flowers are growing out of it."

Bob Hutton, in from Hollywood, danced with his ex-wife, Natalie Thompson, at El Morocco . . . A group of models leaving today to fly down to Rio for a fashion show . . . Vicente Gomez, great Spanish guitarist at Cafe Society Uptown, just got out of the army. J. Edgar Hoover once sent him a letter of thanks for a benefit show, and Gomez felt he had been so honored, the least he could do was enlist . . . Leon Enken now admits 51.

Al Schacht will open a new restaurant next door to the Ambassador Hotel . . . Mike Porter, former editor, has taken over the Sands Point Riviera Beach Club, Port Washington, and reopens it next month . . . Paul Martin joins the Russell Birdwell publicity office . . . That's earl, brother.

Procedure For Haines Cheesecake Pics

Left—Songstress Connie Haines takes time out for a session with her makeup man before going in front of the camera.

Center—It's only Lou Costello's cameras—but even then, cheesecake plays an important part in the life of a radio canary (ya gotta look pretty as well as sing pretty, for some reason) and Connie is quite willing to oblige.

Right—The most satisfying results—with a change of poses and bathing suits. Connie is with the Bud Abbott and Lou Costello show.

FEMININITY IS EXEMPLIFIED by diminutive Connie Haines, warbler on Abbott-Costello's NBC Comedy fest. Anything with ruffles is good style and Connie's white Lobster blouse boasts eyelet-embroidered frills.

Connie Haines Sings For Patients

SONGSTRESS CONNIE HAINES, accompanied by guitar-strumming Pfc Warren Boden, toured the wards at EOH last week during her appearance at the Steel Pier. Here's Connie giving out for a trio of Haddon Hall's 2nd floor patients, left to right, Pfc Charles Wright, of Worcester, Mass.; Pvt. Fred Friget, of Brooklyn, N. Y., and S/Sgt. Walter Oman, of Troy, N. Y.

NOW in Person

The CHARIOTEERS

CONNIE HAINES
SINGING STAR OF THE ABBOTT & COSTELLO RADIO SHOW

JOE, LOU and ARLENE CAITES

EXTRA ADDED ATTRACTION!

JACKIE GLEASON Comedy Star of "FOLLOW THE GIRLS"

ADAMS

ON STAGE THURS. The INK SPOTS · ELLA FITZGERALD · COOTIE WILLIAMS and All-STAR SEPIA REVUE and his ORCHESTRA

Connie Haines and Bob Matthews (top left and right), singing stars of "The Abbott & Costello Radio Show," head the giant stage bill playing for the last times today at the State Theater. Co-headlined is Adrian Rollini...

Connie Haines, Star of Opening Show at Adams Theater Aug. 30

"I wear American Shops clothes and love their Hollywood style," says Connie Haines

NEW YORK, N. Y.—A bright star in the all-star stage show planned for the grand re-opening of the Adams Theater on Thursday, August 30th, is Connie Haines, one of America's favorite movie and radio songbirds. Connie has just completed a long radio run with the Abbott and Costello show and is transferring a tour of the nation's stages.

Connie Haines chooses American Shops' suits because she likes their movieland design. Tailored in the California mode, the new Fall dressmaker and man-tailored suits are considered tops in fashion by experts.

The explanation is simple . . . . Hollywood style expert checks the designs preferred by the stars and then tailors every new detail into the new dressmaker and man-tailored suits sold by that big store.

Famous people like Martha Scott, Jane Wyatt, Arlene Francis, Martha Tilton and others who wear American Shops clothes say they like the styles because they have that "movie-star look." Every garment is made up in 100% pure wool. The suits are dramatic, different and priced as low as $24.95. Charge and budget privileges are extended. The American Shops is located at 800 Broad street next to the Newsreel Theater in Newark, N. J. Open nightly excepting Tuesdays and Thursdays. No connection with any other store of similar name.

"I wear American Shops clothes and love their Hollywood style," says Connie Haines

NEW YORK, N. Y.—Her real name is Yvonne Marie JaMais, but band leader Harry James rechristened her "Connie Haines" while the trio were riding in a cab to play a dance engagement at the Benjamin Franklin Hotel in Philadelphia, back in 1939. She started out to be a dancer . . . and wound up one of America's top flight singing stars.

Connie signed with Tommy Dorsey after singing with the James orchestra for three months, and later joined the Abbott & Costello radio show in Hollywood.

Connie Haines chooses American Shops suits because she likes their movieland design. Tailored in the California mode, the new Fall dressmaker and man-tailored suits are considered tops in fashion by experts.

The explanation is simple . . . . Hollywood style expert checks the designs preferred by the stars and then tailors every new detail into the new dressmaker and man-tailored suits sold by that big store.

Famous people like Martha Scott, Jane Wyatt, Arlene Francis, Martha Tilton and others who wear American Shops clothes say they like the styles because they have that "movie-star look." Every garment is made up in 100% pure wool. The suits are dramatic, different and priced as low as $24.95. Charge and budget privileges are extended. The American Shops is located at 800 Broad street next to the Newsreel Theater in Newark, N. J. Open nightly excepting Tuesdays and Thursdays. No connection with any other store of similar name.

DO IT YOURSELF

☆

LOVELY CONNIE HAINES, N.B.C.'s petite singer on the popular Abbott and Costello air show, illustrates the MUSTS in a busy career girl's life . . . Richard of Wilshire Center, well known beauty consultant of Los Angeles, says, "Do it yourself, if you are too busy for an appointment at your beauty salon, but do it correctly" . . .

☆

....UPPER....

DON'T PATCH YOUR MANICURE . . . Remove the polish with an oil re- mover . . . Soften your cuticle in warm water and gently massage it with oil or cuticle cream . . This will strengthen nails and prevent breaking . . . Dry the nails and first apply a good base coat for a smooth surface . . . then a light first coat of polish . . . Your sec- ond coat is applied a little heavier . . . Last use one of the many magical, in- stant-drying liquids so that there will be no more smudged nails, nor long intervals of waiting until the nails are thoroughly dry . . . Regardless of the success of your home manicure, how- ever, a regular appointment at your beauty salon is advisable in order to keep the hands looking their best . . .

☆

....CENTER....

WHETHER A PERMANENT WAVE, na- trally curly hair or straight hair brush- ing will give new life and greater beauty to your hair . . . When you brush, get a firm grip and use a roll- ing or rotating movement from scalp to the ends of the hair . . . Faithful brushing will not only enhance hair beauty but will assure you lovelier hair-dos, since well conditioned hair has more elasticity and works much easier in the hands of your hair dresser . . .

☆

....LOWER....

BEAUTIFUL, LUSTROUS HAIR . . . a rad- iant smile, and Connie Haines steps from her dressing room to captivate you with her charm and singing . . .

Costello and Company Wow Diamond Gloves Audience

By Pete R

It was a killer diller! It was wonderful! It was terrific! It was stupendous!

All of which is a mere understatement of what 8,000 Paterson citizens had served to them on a Diamond Gloves dish at the fourth session of the 1945 tournament at Hinchliffe Stadium last night.

What a Night!

The punch festival at last evening left the fans limp for it was featured as one of the finest programs of entertainment any assemblage of Diamond Glovers has witnessed in the history of the years of the classic.

Hearts a fthose present went into the ring as the city's son, comedian Lou Costello vaulted over the top rope to roll to the center of the canvas. The crowd also paid tribute to former lightweight champion Benny Leonard and the men he fought in championship contests. Lew Tendler, who they preceded the popular comedian by a matter of about four bouts. Men in the Maritime Service, including a number of officers and heroes home again on visits to their families were given ovations.

Costello Party

Accompanying the Universal motion picture star to Paterson and in his party were his sister, Marie, who is married to Joe Kirk, who ad-libbed in the ring with Lou: Connie Haines who sang "My Dreams Are Getting Better All The Time" and "Good, Good, Good," Bob Matthews who rendered "Star Dust" and "Dreams;" Milton "Professor" Melonhead. Lou's brother, Pat, and wife, his aunt and uncle, Mr. and Mrs. Michael Cavallo and Mr. and Mrs. Peter Stevens.

Coming into the Stadium, Costello went out of his way to say hello to Mrs. Sadie Fidler Weinert, secretary of the Recreation Commission, whom he knew from back in his athletic days. Mrs. Weinert was accompanied by her husband.

Costello Wows 'Em

After Costello had recovered —'A?:'.. -Greer... -... a Franklin began lifting a baby Grand Piano into the ring and Lou went over to volunteer his assistance. He waved his hand to the piano movers in the direction of the center of the ring. Then he bounced off the ropes.

Connie Haines said "I don't blame Lou for raving about Paterson after seeing all these wonderful people." She also warmed the hearts of the multitude with her enthusiasm and the manner in which she performed, winning acclaim with her charm and beauty. The ladies in the Costello party were presented with floral bouquets.

Accompanying the vocalists on the piano through the courtesy of the Colonial Inn, Bill Olmstead did a smart job.

The entire Costello party was called into the ring where all posed for a photograph. Lou remarked that hes had two sweethearts in Paterson, one about 10 years old and the other 6, Marie and Ronnie Greene. The crowd yelled for them to get into the ring. Lou took the younger daughter of the Associate Editor of the News and President of the National Boxing Association to the "mike" and said "I asked you to marry me tonight and what did you say?" Little Ronnie drew laughs with a decided "No."

34 Brings Luck To Connie Haines

Thirty-four is a lucky number for Connie Haines, singing star of Abbott and Costello's Radio Show, now appearing in person at the Roxy. In that year she came here and won first prize in the Fred Allen Amateur Contest—$100 and a week at the Roxy. During the run she occupied dressing room No. 34, the same room she uses today.

SOUTHERNER... Connie Haines sings with a Southern drawl on stage at the Roxy in the Abbott and Costello show, between screenings of "Nob Hill."

Connie Haines has turned from her usual spot of name-band singer and is making her first New York appearance as a featured tunestress with Abbott and Costello on the Roxy stage.

GEORGE RAFT JOAN BENNETT VIVIAN BLAINE Peggy ANN GARNER
NOB HILL in Technicolor
20.
Doors Open 10:00 A.M.

IN PERSON on stage
BUD ABBOTT — LOU COSTELLO
With Their Entire Radio Gang
CONNIE HAINES And Other Big Acts

ROXY 7th Ave. & 50th Street

Abbott, Costello On Roxy Stage, And Very Funny

By FRANK QUINN

For the countless fans who have paid homage to the nation's top comedy team of films and the airwaves, the Roxy stars Abbott and Costello in person.

The local date starts the personal appearance tour of the comics and all revenue will benefit the Lou Costello, Jr. Foundation being established to combat juvenile delinquency.

All the radio gang are on the program, including "Prof" Melonhead, Bob Mathews, Milt Bronson and Joe Kirk. Abbott and Costello convulse with their most popular routine, "Who's on First." This is one of those skits that will live in memory.

Connie Haines, Bud & Lou's radio songbird, is an added attraction. This pert singer chirps a few choruses of popular ballads in swell style. Also on the bill are the Hermanos Williams Trio, in rhythmic precision acrobatics. The Roxyettes perform the thrilling walking-ball routine.

Motion Picture Daily (NEW YORK CITY)

JUL 6 - 1945

Final Times Square Bond Show Today

The final of a series of daily war bond rallies which the industry staged at its head booth at the Times Square Statue of Liberty will take place today when the entire Roxy stage show featuring Abbott and Costello, with Connie Haines and Bob Mathews, will be presented, in addition to a special farewell show with Lucy Monroe, Phil Brito, Diane Courtney, Cass Franklin, Norman Lawrence, Blaine Shannon, Nord Cornell, Don Romero and Vicki Vola.

Betty Grable to Appear At Yankee Stadium

Betty Grable will make a long-awaited appearance in New York City tonight at Yankee Stadium, where the Army Ground Forces will stage a demonstration, Here's Your Infantry. Admission to the giant show will be only by the purchase of War Bonds, now on sale at moving picture theaters in all boroughs and Westchester.

Also scheduled to be on hand for the event are Edward Arnold, Helen Hayes, Lucille Ball, Dennis Morgan, Judy Canova, Hoagy Carmichael, Helen Jepson, Leo Carrillo, Edgar Kennedy and Connie Haines.

3rd and FINAL WEEK!
GEORGE RAFT
JOAN BENNETT
VIVIAN BLAINE
Peggy Ann GARNER
NOB HILL
IN TECHNICOLOR
with ALAN REED
20.
IN PERSON! ON STAGE!
BUD ABBOTT — LOU COSTELLO
With Their Entire Radio Gang Including
JOE KIRK · PROFESSOR MELONHEAD
BOB MATHEWS · MILT BRONSON
HERMANOS WILLIAMS TRIO
Extra! CONNIE HAINES
Lovely Singing Star of The Abbott & Costello Radio Show
COOL ROXY 7th Ave. & 50th Street
DOORS OPEN 10 A.M.

Senate Vote o[...]

Continued from Page 1

tried to get an agreement for the vote tomorrow.

Morse objected at that time, but later withdrew his protest.

Tom Eisdale flattered a guy twi...lls size at a 3rd Avenue ... for using "ungentlemanly six"... Brian Donlevy left a new ... The Big town makes him soon nervous ... Connie Haines has returned by the Coast where she may take a Summer radio replacement... Annie Sheridan is due in town

CELEBRITY PARTY SUN. NITE JULY 22 HONORING
RADIO'S SINGING TOAST FROM COAST TO COAST

CONNIE
HAINES
NOW APPEARING AT THE ROXY, PLUS
EDDIE
DAVIS
THE NATION'S No. 1 SINGING HOST

RELAX *in your* SLACKS *for* DINNER *&* SHOW *at* AIR-COOLED
LEON & EDDIE'S 33 W 52

POPULAR
SERIES
3006
50c PLUS TAX

TWO SMASH HITS BY LOVELY
CONNIE HAINES
"CALIFORNIA SUNBEAM"
Jumpy, Jivey, Terrific!
"SHE'S FUNNY THAT WAY"
A Heart Throb

MERCURY RECORDS

Della Norrell's quit pro war-
bling to be Mrs. Andy Russell.
Happy couple and Connie Haines.

THE Hollywood REP(

Guesting

Today
Louis Jourdan with George Fisher on
"Hollywood Spotlight," KECA, 2:45
p.m.
Connie Haines with Mauri Cliffer on
"Teen and Twenty Time," KMPC,
5:05 p.m.

Rhythm Show

"Rhapsody in Rhythm," a sparkling
new Sunday musical program over
NBC, offers the smooth vocal artistry
of Connie Haines, the flying fingers of
pianist Skitch Henderson, the well-
woven harmonies of the Golden Gate
Quartet and the velvet musical patterns
of Jan Savitt and the Top-Hatters.

CONNIE HAINES back in Hollywood
after theatre tour.

Above: Connie Haines,
Robert Walker, Peter
Lawford and Martha
Stewart at the Duke
Ellington opening at
Ciro's, famed nicery.

CONNIE HAINES is the girl, Sammy Kaye is the object of her af-
fections. Connie, a Capitol artist
is clicking big on her own. Sammy
and his bandsmen move into the
Palladium Feb. 8 for at least a
week run following Harry James'
music.

RECORDATA: Glenn Miller moves
to the top at Bluebird this week with
his "Fools Rush In" and "Yours Is
My Heart Alone." Former features
Ray Eberle, while the latter is a
straight instrumental. Earl Hines'
work at the piano brings his "Deep
Forest" and "Lightly and Politely"
into the second place.... "I'm Nobody's Baby" backed with "Buds
Won't Bud" as handled by Tommy
Dorsey takes all honors at Victor.
Connie Haines, a newcomer to the
band, handles the vocals, and does a
very good job... The same two tunes,
all sung by Judy Garland, take top
honors at Decca, with "You're Lonely" and "Fools Fall In Love" by Tony
Martin a close runner-up.... Frankie

Connie Haines to Sing
In Main Street Church

Miss Connie Haines, radio vocalist, will sing tonight at the
Main Street Baptist church, where
the Jacksonville Baptist Training
Union association will hold its
quarterly mass meeting at 7:30
o'clock.

Miss Haines, a native of Jacksonville, was spotted by Abbott
and Costello about five years ago.
She was featured singer on their
program until a few weeks ago
when she secured her release to
make records and personal appearances. She has devoted about
80 per cent of her time to USO,
hospital and camp show work
during the war, and did scores of
overseas broadcasts. Miss Haines
has been very active in church
work since she was a child, and
gives 10 per cent of her income
to her church.

...an, and Mrs. Johnny DeVoogt and Mrs. Clint Davis, wives ...James band members. (5) Georgia Gibbs sings a sad one, ...d with feeling, on the Sunday Philco hour. (6) Pvt. Bob ...onnelly dates with his fave vocalist, Connie Haines, and ...andleaders Tony Pastor and Frankie Carle at the Palla-...um. (7) Fred Waring, who lunches here in his Broadway ...ffice, may be taking his meals at his country club, Shawnee-...-Delaware Inn in Pennsylvania if plans for his new NBC ...ries (starting June 4) go through. Two of the daily half-hour ...ows may be aired from the Inn.

KAY KYSER WAS original "editor" of "G.I. Journal," still makes frequent appearances on show. Little Connie Haines sings an original song at each "pressing." Men from overseas are the composers.

Page Twenty-eight

At Roxy

Connie Haines, above, new singing star, is appearing with Abbott and Costello at the Roxy Theatre. She formerly was featured vocalist with Harry James and Tommy Dorsey's bands and now is offering de luxe renditions of "Autumn Serenade," "No Can Do" and "I Don't Care Who Knows It."

7. Jewelry continues to gleam in the fashion limelight and Connie Haines, petite NBC songstress, goes formal with dog-collar of tiny pearls combined with black velvet ribbon and a bracelet of these lustrous little gems.

MECHANICSBURG, PA. LOCAL NEWS
Cir. D. 1,640

JUL 26 1945

In order to have a week to "break in" their routine for their scheduled 3-week personal appearance at New York's Roxy Theatre beginning July 3, Abbott and Costello and their entire cast principals will go to New York for their final broadcast of the season, Thursday, June 28, over NBC. Bud Abbott (above) and Lou Costello (below) will bring along their regular troupe, including Songstress Connie Haines and Singer Bob Matthews.

Roaming Bullets, Connie Haines, Buster Sherwood, June Hutton and Jimmy Dorsey.

Connie Haines

BILLBOARD (CINCINNATI, OHIO)
Cir. 31,347

Roxy, New York
(Reviewed Wednesday Afternoon, July 4)

New Roxy bill supporting Bob still doesn't really get going until the midway point. Until then, Abbott and Costello, assisted by Joe Kirk for one bit, go thru the stale "fighting" routine for a few laughs and A. & C. come next out the old switch on the vince-square-foot story. This they handle very well, C. doing himself especially proud as a pennant-in-shasak. But it sort of peters out and Bob Mathews, working from the sky show, is not strong enough to keep the pace going. Mathews reveals a good larynx, nice stage presence and okay delivery but has styled himself so heartily in the crooner tradition, plus gobs of schmaltz, that his act runs downhill.

Show gets a powerful shot in the arm from next number, teaming the dancing ensemble and Hermaine Williams Trio. Production is built around Salon and is novelty done. Number is a lesson in what can be accomplished with simple hangings plus imagination in the use of lighting. The usual wonderful Roxy conglmeratous help, of course. Themselves does bang-up hoofing job on Latin patterns and number segues into the acrobatic trio. Tumblers are in top form and draw a sock hand.

Costello returns with Professor Melonhead, also from the sky show. The pair proceed to yank belly-laughs out of the scob with their standard wood-difficulties. Routine reaches its high point when they start smashing crackers and spewing them at each other and receive its topper when Paul Ash cue men raise colored umbrellas. That should have been the exit bit Melonhead stays on for a mild, self-cigaret bit. Altogether, however, it's meaty vaude stuff.

Connie Haines—clad in a gown that makes her look like she's being pushed by a closed—follows to thrush two numbers and a ballad. The ballad is creepy but the tempo tunes are sock, especially the second, A Kiss Goodnight, which she sold to a fare-the-well.

Gal could have stayed on for more but instead enters the line in The Roxy's standard ball-walking routine. Number has the usual quota of real and fake spills and nets top splitting.

A. & C. close with the old parley routine built around "Who," "That," "Why," the baseball version. Feller is sure-fire and pair handles it like the release they are, but routine runs much too long and desperately needs a climax. As it stands, it stops abruptly when A. & C. bow and powder off, leaving crowd high and dry. Liner when caught.

Paul Ross.

Connie Haines and Jan Savitt Top 'Rhapsody in Rhythm' Talent List

HOLLYWOOD — Little Connie Haines is a singing star now — she's on NBC's "Rhapsody in Rhythm."

Connie owes her success to her mother, who was her first teacher. Her rise to the top rank of radio vocalists has paralleled that of Frank Sinatra and other outstanding singers. Connie and Frank were teammates in the Harry James and Tommy Dorsey bands.

Connie is one of the tiniest glamor girls in radio—she is five feet tall, and tips the beam at 100 pounds. The blue-eyed brunette was born in Savannah, Ga., Jan. 20, 1922. She received encouragement and training from her mother, a prominent vocal teacher, and made her air debut when she was four years old. After several years of radio as a child prodigy, her first trip to New York was rewarded with a contract at the Roxy Theater. Engagements with the James and Dorsey bands followed, and then a series of night club appearances, finally leading to her vocal spot on NBC's "Abbott and Costello" show.

During the past season, Connie took a vacation, then appeared at New York's finest supper clubs, and has just returned to Hollywood and "Rhapsody in Rhythm" (NBC Sundays, 10:30 p.m.). This show is a summer replacement for "Meet Me at Parky's," which resumes Sept. 15.

Providing the music for the same program is the popular maestro, Jan Savitt. Although Jan's childhood ambition was to become a scientist, the attraction of music won out. Jan, son of the bandmaster of the Imperial Regimental Band of Czar Nicholas, was born in St.

Editors:

Included in this service, although not shown on this page, are half-column mats of Jan Savitt, Bernie West and Happy Felton.

Also, please note that the world premiere of "Sunday in Brooklyn" by Elie Siegmeister, scheduled for the NBC Symphony Orchestra on July 14, will be presented instead on July 21. Story on premiere appeared in June 21 issue of NBC News Features.

GEORGIA GAL—Petite Connie Haines from Savannah, Ga., is featured vocalist of NBC's "Rhapsody in Rhythm," which replaces the "Meet Me At Parky's" program during the summer.

VARIETY

SHORT SHORTS

PLANTED

Metro

Eddie Abdo, Yussef Ali, Eugene Borden, David Cota; "Yolanda and the Thief."

Eddie Acuff, Chester Clute, Joe Dumeda, Shimen Ruskin, "For Better, For Worse."

Paramount

Will Wright, Milton Kibbee, Hary Hayden, Harry Barris, Roberta Jonay, Mae Busch, Gloria Williams, "The Blue Dahlia."

Columbia

Robert Keane, George Carleton, Vera Hruba Ralston will star in the picture.

Dick Hyland has been signed by PRC to screenplay "I Ring Doorbells," which Martin Mooney produces.

NEW CONTRACTS

Lew Landers has been signed by Alexander-Stern to direct "Arson Squad" for PRC release.

STORY BUYS

"Flight From Youth," magazine yarn by William A. Barrett, purchased by Metro.

LOCATIONING

"The Bandit of Sherwood Forest" returned to the Simi Valley location yesterday after four days indoors due to rain.

Lloyd Bacon heads tomorrow for Louisiana and thence to Florida, for swamp scenes to be used as background footage for 20th-Fox's "Enchanted Voyage."

TITLE CHANGE

"The Plainsman and the Lady," from "Glory Road," Republic.

BIRTHS

Twin Daughters were born to Mrs. Michael Dowd at Queen of Angels hospital Monday night. Father is vocalist with Kay Kyser's orchestra.

Daughter, weighing five pounds, 13½ ounces, to Mrs. Andy Potter, March 27 at Glendale Research hospital. Father is producer of KFI's "Everybody's Favorite" program. The newcomer has been named Andra Lynn.

From debut and singing star Paramount production, "Stork Club." Tune is being published by Peer International with English lyrics by Al Stewart.

"Oh, My Achin' Back," the Fred Astaire-Money Amsterdam GI ditty recently recorded by Tony Romano for American Recording Co., has been published by Feist and set for nationwide exploitation campaign.

"There's No You," song by Hal Hopper of the Pied Pipers singing group, published by the Barton Music Co. of New York. Sheet music arrived on west coast stands this week.

Larry Douglas will feature "You Belong To My Heart" from Disney's "Three Caballeros" in the "Here To Romance" show over CBS.

Connie Haines yesterday took over for ailing Martha Raye on album for the Armed Forces Radio Service.

De Sylva Inks Currier

Mary Currier inked with B. G. De Sylva yesterday to play the role of Sherman. Billingsley's wife in "The Stork Club."

Walter Winchell
In New York
(Copyright, 1946, by The Hearst Corporation.)

Moonlight Over the Hudson

Silhouettes in the Night: Walter Pidgeon and Frank Sinatra (who have about 40 million young fans between them) spellbound by a middle-aged woman's conversation in the Waldorf foyer....Gene Raymond, back from the wars, getting sighs from the Embassy's hatcheck banditti...Connie Haines wearing a gold-and-ruby dog collar—and her pooch wearing her poils...Mrs. Ray Bolger bawling out the Duke and Duchess of Sutherland for arriving at her groom-a-hit ("Three to Make Ready") at 9:30...Ex-Ambassador J. P. Kennedy on E. 50th street telling a copyogist that the stories of his "cornering the market in Scotch" are exaggerated...Louise Allbritton's "Palm Springs tan"—in the Stork...Belle Livingston, attractively gray, reminiscing about her prohibition heydey at a 47th street bar...Lovely Loretta Young at the Wedgwood Room...Sec'y Byrnes (at a party in the Hampshire House) toasting Gromyko: "Those whom war hath brought together—let no peace put asunder!"

POPULAR SERIES
3006
50c PLUS TAX

TWO SMASH HITS BY LOVELY

CONNIE HAINES

"CALIFORNIA SUNBEAM"
Jumpy, Jivey, Terrific!

"SHE'S FUNNY THAT WAY"
A Heart Throb

MERCURY RECORDS

Mercury...

grabbed off Buddy Rich, Eileen Barton, Rose Marie, Rex Stewart, Buddy Morrow, Vincent Lopez, Chuck Foster, Connie Haines, and Frank Parker in a big expansion program.

ROBERT DANA, "World-Telegram," says
"The Funniest and Cleanest Comedy I've Seen This Season in a Night Club"

JOEY ADAMS
MARK PLANT - TONY CANZONERI

• EXTRA ADDED ATTRACTION •

CONNIE HAINES
SINGING STAR OF ABBOTT & COSTELLO PROGRAM

SHOWS—8:30-12:15-2:15.

Paris to New Orleans

LA MARTINIQUE
57 W. 57
PLaza 5-4754

"G. I. Journal"...

(Continued from Page 24)

as an authentic testing ground for the jokes.

Even before our men started coming back from overseas, AFRS was getting reports on what the men did and didn't like by way of radio humor. Now, the writers of the Journal (formerly top scripters for stars like Benny, Bergen, and Burns and Allen) evolve their funny remarks and if they're in doubt as to their "socko," they still leave the lines in and let the men at the Canteen decide.

If the boys laugh long and hard, the gag stays in. If it flops, out it goes. This convenient manner of grading gags is made possible by a show-saving feature — editing — which puts a Journal production on a basis similar to movies.

For a half-hour comedy script like this one, there should be several hours' rehearsal to assure a smooth and Kay Kyser. Kay played for the program for more than ten weeks, and when he was called out of town to do camp appearances, Bing Crosby stepped in as "editor." When Bing went on tour, his "son," Bob Hope, took over, followed by Jack Carson. Since then on, these four stars have tried to rotate as editors of the Journal.

After the first few months, the show outgrew the studio at Radio recorders and it moved to Columbia Square. But something was haywire. The scripts, written especially each week by two top men whose style just suited the stars appearing, didn't seem to hit the mark. The gags fell flat before a civilian audience which didn't seem to get the point of the jokes. Producer Frank O'Connor (Sgt. at AFRS) wondered if the problem might be solved by giving the show to the Canteen. The same script that had played to a big farce at CBS waxed the G.I. at the service center.

...only the canned crowd »
At the

spots were recorded before a live audience. Music was recorded at the studio and added when the entire program was "assembled." Corp. Jim Burton, who succeeded Sgt. O'Connor as producer, felt that the audience was really being cheated. So, Lieut. Jimmy Grier was asked to present his Coast Guard band on the program. When Jimmy went overseas, Dick Aurandt became music editor and each week has a wonderful time dreaming up special touches for the now-complete edition.

Sings Original Number

An added attraction of each Friday night's "cutting" is a number by petite Connie Haines, who sings the original song of the week—a song written by a serviceman overseas. Hundreds of exceptionally good songs have been received. When Connie's busy schedule doesn't permit her to make her usual appearance at the Canteen, she goes to a recording session with Major Meredith Willson and the AFRS orchestra, and the result is a perfect version of some aspiring songwriter's dream child.

Connie's a serious young girl. She'll probably expect you to marry her and raise a family. Maybe as many as three children.

Mel: Th-th-three children? But I'm an ar-ar-army ma-ma—I'm a sold-sold-sold—Oh, what the heck! That's thirty-six points, anyway!

Besides Bing, Hope, Carson, and Kay, other editors who've blue-penciled the Journal have been: Bill Bendix, Jack Haley, Monty Woolley, Jack Benny, Burns and Allen, Frank Morgan, Judy Canova, Robert Benchley, Edgar Bergen and Charlie McCarthy, Milton Berle, Bette Davis, Red Skelton, Roy Rogers, and Orson Welles.

Buddy Rich, Others Ink Record Pacts

Chicago — The Buddy Rich band, which has been coming right along since the time Sinatra put some 2&0's into the venture, snared a contract with Mercury records that will find Rich's discs on the market almost by the time this is read.

Dottie Reid and the drummer-leader will handle the vocals on several tunes not selected at this writing.

Other artists signed by record firms were the new Bobby Byrne band with Owen Vincent Lopez band, singer Connie Haines and the Four Vagabonds by Mercury, John Kirby joining Benny Carter on the DeLuxe label, Kitty Kallen, ex-James and JD sharp with Musicraft, as well as the Fontaine Sisters (Bea, Marge and Jerry) at a one-year deal with Musicraft.

Connie Haines Club Organized in City

A group of Jacksonville Teen-agers have gotten together and organized a "Connie Haines Fan Club" for the former Jacksonville girl who is really going places with her singing, bearing in mind that she would appreciate letters from the home-towners letting her know they are following her progress.

Miss Joanne Carver of — Ridgewood Road is the president of this club, which was organized in April, and she requests all teenagers who are interested in becoming members to contact her. They also plan to publish a small paper which will carry items of interest to members. This paper will be published once a month.

Recognized everywhere as a singer whose talents have registered a new high.

Starting October on the ABBOTT-COSTELLO RADIO PROGRAM FOR CAMEL CIGARETTES
Coast to Coast
Recording Artist

Many thanks to all my friends who have made my personal appearance tour successful, also those who helped me in the past.

Exclusive Management
MUSIC CORPORATION OF AMERICA
LONDON • NEW YORK • CHICAGO
SAN FRANCISCO • BEVERLY HILLS
CLEVELAND • DALLAS

THE CAPITOL

— Nightlife: —

It's Laugh Season At the Martinique
By LEE MORTIMER

I discovered that critics can laugh out loud, at the Martinique opening, when some of the boys burst into guffaws at the madcap comedy in the show.

Joey Adams and his gang—Mark Plant and Tony Canzoneri sparkplug the 8 and 12 o'clock editions. Charlie Carlisle, a highly touted funny man from Detroit, wows 'em at the 2 o'clock revue.

Adams has gone a long way since I discovered (ahem!) him at Leon & Eddie's, where he worked for peanuts. He now rates a bagful—caked in gold. With handsome Plant, of the glorious voice, and little Tony who is again a champ, as a straight man, Joey has whipped up an act that no one ever topped at La Martinique, or many other places.

Carlisle is a clever guy who starts out cold and grows on you. He was hampered opening night trying to get the feel of a eighteen audience, but came through with genuine humor and comedy skill.

Delores Gray having walked out of the show before its opening, the prexus audience was denied a gal singer. That song-

... hit has now been added—personable and lovely-voiced Connie Haines, of the radio.

Phil Wayne and his good musicians tickle with the tunes and Phil briefly joins Adams and

Resounding Smack Given Jax GI By Connie Haines

When the transport Alcoa Patriot docked at San Pedro harbor, Calif. last week, two Jaxons were very pleasantly surprised—Connie Haines of the Abbott and Costello show and Sgt. Jack Humphries, who was among the 2,000 soldiers returning on the boat from the South Pacific and about to be discharged.

Petite Miss Haines, in her rounds of doing patriotic entertainment, had risen early to meet the incoming ship so as to sing in welcome to the high-point GIs on their return to the States. As her golden voice soared over the public address system to the happy boatload of soldiers, one was particularly interested in the song and more especially its singer. He was Sergeant Humphries.

Pushing his way to the microphone from which Connie was working, the tanned sergeant rushed to see her former Andrew Jackson High school mate that the broke her ring right then and there and gave Humphries a big embrace and kiss!

Incidentally, it has just been learned that the four-foot-eleven, 96-pound Miss Haines proved herself a hero this past summer when spending a short vacation between hospital and theatre appearances. While eating at Oak Spring Harbor, Long Island, the boat on which she was a passenger overturned and Connie rescued Don drowning a 200-pound man!

SOUTHERNER . . . Connie Haines sings with a Southern drawl on stage at the Roxy in the Abbott and Costello show, between screenings of "Nob Hill."

Noel Wesley, former Hollywood producer has set up offices in the Kardi building where he is planning an intimate musical revue called "Here Comes The Showboat," a story of a young theatrical troupe on a showboat playing up and down the Ohio River.

Connie Haines, singing star of the Abbott and Costello radio show, has signed for the lead role, that of singing mistress of ceremonies on the showboat, with the proviso that she will be let out, if she is called to make another picture.

Billie Bryant of "Showboat" fame will assist in the writing of the script. Paul Girard of Ringling Brothers circus will stage the musical numbers.

ARMED FORCES RADIO SERVICE

Art Tatum, George Union, and the Mello Larks in "Jubilee's For Fun" etc.," tonight, CBS.

radio riffs

Connie Haines goes back on the air with Abbott and Costello October 4 for the fourth successive year.

ROXY

Bud Abbott

Lou Costello

"Connie is one of the tiniest glamour girls in radio—she is four feet, eleven inches tall and tips the scales at 100 pounds. Connie Haines' thrushing on NBC goes for 'Curtain Calls.'" Walter Winchell's column, *New York Daily Mirror*, December, 1945, and following up, "Connie Haines, the radio thrush, is a new threat for the juke box crown. Her soon due disc is tagged: 'California Sunbeam'" May 6, 1946.

Variety, June 19, 1946: Connie Haines in "Rhapsody In Rhythm" show mooned fetchingly (to Skitch Henderson's piano and band), singing "They Say It's Wonderful."

Robert Coleman—*The Theatre* column reported "Miss Connie Haines is in Hollywood for a radio show and a role in the 'Bloomer Girl' film at Universal."

The Hollywood Reporter, Oct.17. 1947: "Benny Fields and Connie Haines, appearing on the same bill at Hotel El Rancho Vegas, are noted to be the year's greatest entertainment daily double value."

The Columbus, Ohio *Sentinel* says: "Diminutivness in an attractive young miss draws such phrases as 'cute little package' and 'petite.' But, Connie Haines, singer on the Abbott & Costello radio show, would trade her 4 feet 11 inches any day for something taller. Accommodations must be made for her in all her professional work, such as a special microphone or other adjustments for the radio, and devious methods of increasing her height for still and motion pictures.

In private life Connie has similar problems, having to stand on a stool to reach kitchen cupboards. When she dances with a tall man she has to peek under his arm to see where she is going. She can't find sophisticated enough dresses for her small figure and must have her clothes specially made. All those efforts, however, failed, especially when she is at the microphone with Will Osborne the 6 feet 5 inch conductor of the Abbott & Costello show."

MORE TOURING AND THE MOVIES

In the year that followed, Connie completed three motion pictures, cut a number of new recordings, and made frequent guest appearances on radio shows that included Bob Hope, Frank Sinatra, Hoagy Carmichael,

Skitch Henderson, Andy Russell, Jan Savitt, Kay Kyser, Jackie Gleason, Sammy Kaye, Mel Tormé, Mickey Rooney, Helen Forrest, and Bing Crosby.

A special moment for her happened one Sunday morning during services in a chapel at the Air Transport Command post in Long Beach, California. It was the very first time a Hollywood personality had been invited to participate in a military Sunday service.

Connie was in her element. She had sung for Billy Graham in his Youth for Christ movement on several occasions, a great experience for the twenty-three year old entertainer.

"Colleen Townsend, a new hot property at Fox, and I, flew to Chicago with Billy Graham for a large rally. Naturally, when Colleen made the decision to leave the world of entertainment and give her life to God, it made front-page news. In those days, women ministers had not yet 'arrived,' and Colleen had decided to focus on Christian education."

With Van Johnson singing "Choo Choo, Choo to Idaho" in the Esther Williams film "The Duchess of Idaho". 1949

Upon their arrival in Chicago, the press was waiting: "The questions were unkind. Being a believer in Jesus Christ and unafraid to stand up and say it made you what they called a 'Jesus freak.' One asked her what she thought about the Ingrid Bergman, Roberto Rossellini love affair that had just hit the headlines, and Colleen declared sweetly, 'Let him who is without sin cast the first stone.'"

Singers Andy Russell and Mel Tormé appeared with Connie on a radio show called the Bandwagon. Mel's singing group, The Meltones, were just making respectable musical waves. Then, a return guest appearance on Andy Russell's own show followed a gritty, irritating appearance at the Clover Club on Sunset Boulevard. For Connie it was the good and the bad, all passing through her without negative effect. But the real Connie Haines was steeped in the church singing to servicemen and all that it meant.

"Bullets Durgom introduced me to Joe Pasternak, who cast me in a movie with Esther Williams and Van Johnson called *The Duchess of Idaho*. What a thrill for me when, in the middle of the film, after my scene in the railroad club car dancing and singing 'Choo Choo, Choo to Idaho,' the audience at the Hollywood premiere stood up and bestowed upon me a surprise standing ovation."

Connie always preferred playing herself on screen rather than a particular character in a role. Invariably she was cast as the singer with the band. She thought at the time that acting was being deceptive and phony and could not bring herself to perform accordingly.

Besides those recordings with Harry James and Tommy Dorsey, some of Connie's later successful recordings were "Teasin'," Sonny Burke's "How it Lies, How It Lies," "Mississippi Mud," "Old Man Mose Is Dead," "What is This Thing Called Love?" "You Made Me Love You," and "Will You Still Be Mine," the latter with Teresa Brewer's future husband, Bob Theile of Signature Records, with Ray Block conducting.

When Connie first recorded "Will You Still Be Mine" with Tommy Dorsey, it was the first recording she was allowed to sing solo in her own key. It was, and still stands as, a beautifully phrased performance by a big band singer.

Hollywood became her home. She purchased a vine-covered cottage with a white picket fence in a rural setting for her mother, who shared it with her daughter, Barbara, and her own mother, Nana. Connie took good care of her family, always stating, "What was mine—was theirs. We earned it together."

Every Christmas they congregated in Jacksonville, Florida, for a family reunion to renew themselves in the warmth of family love. "I

With Mickey Rooney at RKO Keith-Boston. 1946.

enjoyed the joy of Daddy John, and all my eight aunts and uncles, not to mention all my cousins."

The Abbott & Costello radio and motion picture job lasted four solid years. "I remember when the boys discovered Dean Martin. It was in a small club in Philadelphia where he was singing. You all know the Dean Martin story. He was a handsome man inside and out."

At the close of the radio show, MGM asked Connie to replace Judy Garland in a theater tour with Mickey Rooney that would take her all around the United States. Judy had been taken ill, so Connie was the natural replacement. She was thrilled, with Judy being her favorite singer. Both girls were short, and even when Connie wore high heels, Mickey remained taller. The voices and vocalizing keys were much the same, so no new arrangements had to be written.

"I was able to sing my own hit records as solos. In my book, Judy was one of the greatest talents of all time. I had seen her every movie and had met her at a birthday party for me given by Lana Turner. To step into Judy's shoes, I would have gladly sung without pay.

"This was just after the end of World War II. On the same bill was the Will Mastin Trio, featuring the eighteen-year-old son, and nephew, Sammy Davis, Jr. Connie and Mickey were both twenty-four year old stars of the show.

"It was a memorable tour. At night, after each show, we had Coca-Cola and hotdog parties. Mickey played the piano and Sammy played drums. In-between, we three would write songs. Mickey was a good songwriter. I wonder what ever happened to those songs? It was on that tour that Mickey and I talked Sammy into singing his first solo on stage. We had to literally drag him out to perform. It was at one of the parties that Sammy sang alone for the first time. He would do impersonations of Frank Sinatra, copying him to a 'T'."

While under contract to Universal Studios, Connie was placed in some Westerns because of her Southern accent. They cast her as a cowgirl. During one of those movies she met a fellow

Connie and Mickey Rooney on tour, 1949.

named Jimmy Dodd. Jimmy later became famous as the television host on the Walt Disney "Mickey Mouse Show." She asked Jimmy and his wife to come over to her house one Sunday evening. She explained that with Jane Russell, Colleen Townsend, Dale and Roy Rogers and Rhonda Fleming she had started what they called the Hollywood Christian Group.

"For some reason, people in show business were frowned upon when they were seen going to church. So we decided to have church in our own homes. What a turn-out we had at our first meeting. They hungered to share their belief in God with others. Few would believe that famous people were just like every other normal person, needing and wanting love and friendship. That Hollywood Christian Group is still going today."

Dale Evans, a former Big Band singer and the wife of the late cowboy star Roy Rogers, recalls it frequently on her TBN-TV weekly show.

Connie Haines kept up her church work while constantly working.

She sang the best she ever sounded at the wedding of her friend Colleen Townsend and Louis Evans, Jr. Louis, like his father, was a minister.

"Since Colleen spent a great deal of time at Fox Studios making pictures, our professional paths did not cross much, but she shines brightly in my memories of those years because of our spiritual rapport and the prayer times we shared—those evenings at friends' houses sponsored each week by our Hollywood Christian Group.

"I look back now at the early years and how I struggled to always do the right thing. In retrospect it seems I was spiritually awkward. Mother had to remind me not to be a fanatic."

"Darling," said her mother, "you know there's a time and place for everything. Some people become uncomfortable when you refer to God, especially at a business meeting."

"Mother, God is my witness even when I sign a contract."

Maybe Connie Haines went too far with refusing to work on Sundays, although the producers were understanding and went along with her, sometimes treating her like a child. She did little to further her career. Church and spiritual work, yes; movies, radio, bands, TV, not much.

"I quit, resigned, left, refused. I turned down offer after offer. I walked out of spots others yearned for, over and over. "

But, nevertheless, and despite the rejections, Connie found herself back smack in the middle of a business career once again.

"It was as if God had pulled me up and shoved me back in."

In her final days of preparation to become an ordained minister, by attending school, Connie was singing better and better. Her career accel-

Two Universal Pictures movie stars Connie Haines and June Haver. (Universal photo)

erated in spite of school and refusing offers. She could have soared to greater heights during this period, perhaps becoming one of the great stars of show business,

"I didn't want that now. Since my vision of Jesus Christ, and since I removed the gun from my father's hand, I have always sung out the message of Him to the world. I was happy being recognized as tops at that."

Harsh Reality

TWO REMARKABLE MEN

DICK GRAY AND BOB DE HAVEN

"I met Bob De Haven when I was nineteen. It was at the Virginia Military Institute Spring Dance. Frank Sinatra, the Pied Pipers and I were singing there with Tommy Dorsey."

Young Bob De Haven was attending Washington and Lee. He had crashed the dance, and, during a break, he went up to Frank and introduced himself, saying, "Frankie boy, you're great. Great, great, great. I'm Bob De Haven. "

"I guess he expected Frank to know him as he knew Frank. As they talked I could not take my eyes off him. Frank must have felt the breeze from my fluttering eyelashes."

Frank introduced Connie to the handsome young man who then turned back to Frank and continued talking.

"I felt quite left out. I stood by, pretending I was hanging on every word, but I was not really listening to them, although I clearly heard my heart beating." Seconds were hours for the young singer.

"Okay then, it's all set. You and the gang come to the frat house tonight, but there's one condition and that is, Connie's my date—okay?"

"What's that?" Frank asked.

"We all went to the fraternity house. Bob arranged it so I had to sit on his lap in the car. Why did I feel this way about a man I had just met? The house mother froze solid when she saw all of us."

"Mom," Bob said, "set eight more places and put another quart of rum in the soup."

Protesting her temperance, Connie immediately realized Bob was just kidding. A fair, blond, debonair and cocky sort of extrovert, Bob De Haven had a English family background and resembled Prince Philip.

"After we parted, I had an ache inside. I wondered when I would see him again. It was a different feeling, not what I had felt for the football stars I dated or the president of the senior class. They were part of fast-moving show business. Bob made time stand still."

Connie Haines and Bob De Haven were not to be married until ten years later. Their romance was tempestuous. Somehow Bob would get to wherever Connie was performing. He would send an orchid on ahead to every venue: a single purple orchid in a box, no card, but the orchid seem to say *Great, Connie, great!* It also said he'd be waiting for her after the show.

"Bob would have to hitchhike from Staunton, Virginia, to where we were appearing, sometimes states away. On the road, I roomed with Jo Stafford and her husband. Jo always gave me that big sister line, 'Don't stay out too late.' But we did."

To Connie, Bob was very exciting, a dynamic and brilliant man, and at the same time just a schoolboy. "Today, I still see his good looks in our daughter, Kim. "

Despite the miles, Bob became Connie's unsteady steady. The two fought frequently because Bob's impulsive ways were both exciting and irritating. They fanned the flames of her emotional nature and equally disturbed her subtle sensibilities. He tried to lead Connie to be as wild, while she tried to tame him. World War II did not help. Bob could now fly to wherever she was performing. He was a whirlwind in uniform. Bob De Haven became an ace in the United States Air Force.

"We'd start out each meeting in each other's arms and end up not talking. First the heat of passion, then the chill of conflict. I felt I was being tempered like steel. Sometimes the breaks away caused me to date other men. Then Bob showed, and there were no other men at all.

"One time, when I returned home in angry tears, Mother gave me that 'Not again!' look, and then the phone rang. I would not answer it. I can't remember how many times it rang that night as I told mother the story of Bob and me. Mother would not let him talk to me even the next day."

Bob barraged Connie with letters while he was on active duty, but she met and dated Dick Gray, a six-foot, wonderful man. Meanwhile, Bob De Haven married another.

"I consider Dick Gray the most fantastic man ever to walk the face of the Earth. Others who knew him agreed. Black hair, deep black eyes, thick eyelashes that tiled gently down, slim jaw line and high cheekbones gave Dick an Oriental look. He was attending the University of Southern California studying to be a chemical engineer."

For Connie, Dick Gray had the wisdom of a man far older than his twenty-four years. Even his father came to him for advice. He was active in the Hollywood Presbyterian Church, where they met. Connie got along well with Dick's parents who confided in her about Dick being adopted. something Dick did not know. Dick worshipped his "parents." Connie and

Dick felt they had the same mission in life, which bound them together. It was a warm, stable, comforting coverlet—far from the emotional roll-coaster experienced with De Haven.

"Our engagement took place within that year in Palm Springs. My mother and his parents were vacationing with us. We drove off, later standing together under a star-filled desert sky with his arms around me. He gently raised my face to his and kissed me tenderly on both eyelids, saying, 'I want you to be my wife, Connie.' Dick was so romantic."

Before she could say a word, he placed a beautiful antique diamond ring on her finger, which she wears to this day. Within a year Dick Gray was dead.

"Right after Dick gave me that ring, he went into the service where he became stricken with a neck ailment that translated into Hodgkins disease, a cancer of the blood. They sent him home from overseas."

Dick's hope for recovery was high, and he cautioned Connie not to fret or inquire about the illness and made her promise to have faith.

This was the time of the Abbott & Costello radio show contract. All other work was set aside. Connie felt a special closeness to Dick Gray. She considered him spiritual royalty. It hurt her deeply to witness his weak-

Connie with Dick Gray, 1946.

ness and sagging spirit as he lost weight, diminishing to one-hundred pounds as they carried him to a hospital, Connie walking beside him.

"You'll get good care here, Dick. You'll gain back your weight and gain back your confidence, don't worry." she hoped.

"I'll gain, if I don't lose you." he said.

"Never." He didn't gain. He lost. At eighty-five pounds, she saw nothing but grimness on the faces of his doctors and his parents. Connie moved into the hospital to be near.

"One night he ordered supper. The nurse brought him a full tray. He seemed cheerful for the moment. He ate well that night and even tried to sing. Dick never sang. We sang all our favorite songs together. Later, I freshened his pillow, kissed him goodnight, and tiptoed out."

Dick Gray never woke up again.

"I grieved and grieved, collapsed, and cried and cried for weeks. I had believed he would be healed. Why did God take him? He brought the love of God to others. Why him and not me? Maybe Dick was needed on another plane to perform even 'higher' work, work that I was not ready for. I prefer to believe that. "

After their engagement, Connie and Dick had talked about their wedding to be. This is what Connie wanted. A happy married life, a good Christian home, even though, with Dick, that home would have been childless.

"What a different life I would have had if he had lived.

"Somehow I felt he was still with me. I could hear him saying, 'Sing out the songs, Connie, and speak the Word.' I was singing them all right, but the songs I was singing were not exactly His word."

Connie moved on with her career, the hope of marriage behind her for the moment. Bob De Haven called to say how sorry he was to hear of Dick's passing. She was happy to hear his voice and was surprised at her mellowness towards him, considering the recent past personality clashes that tore them apart.

"I became engaged to a magnificent man, Norman Waltjen, a Catholic, who, like Bob De Haven, would fly anywhere to be with me after a show. Norman was the son of a former Governor of Maryland. We dated for a while, but we could not cross the religious gap that divided us. It is sad, I guess, how a member of the Catholic Church and a Baptist could be so unbending in their beliefs. Neither would give into the other."

Years later, Connie studied Catholicism and could, in retrospect, better understand Norman's position. For Connie, the differences were now not as important. "We are all God's children," she said.

"For good or for bad, I eloped with Bob De Haven two years after Dick Gray passed on."

One evening when Connie was singing at the Paramount in New York an orchid arrived backstage. No card, but the silence told her it was Bob De Haven saying, "Here I am again."

Bob had mellowed, or so she thought. His marriage had ended just as suddenly as it had begun. De Haven was director of Hughes Aircraft's Flight Test Division. His flair had matured from college dorm to airplane hangar. Their romance took up where it left off.

"Bob De Haven had to come to church if he wanted to date me, because that's where I was. Somewhat reluctantly, he became a part of the church with me. He never had much feeling for the church, but he realized that for me the church came first, and, if he wanted to see me, he had to join in.

"We were getting along fine when he said, 'All right, Connie, I'll take the first step and say that I believe in Jesus Christ.' I was stunned and said, 'Don't say that unless you mean it.' He promised that he meant it, but asked for patience on my part."

The personality clashes were gone, and, although Connie was at first aghast at the idea, they nevertheless rocketed forward together into a Mexico elopement. Her mother was against the sudden churchless marriage, but Connie thought she was ready for love and happiness with the new version of Bob De Haven.

"In my suite in Encinada, Mexico, I remember that I put on a dressy, white taffeta cocktail dress and white matching hat, both adorned with white rose applique petals. When I opened the door, in paraded an entourage of bellboys, waiters, and busboys carrying trays of hors d'oeuvres and buckets of champagne. Eight musicians followed them in, playing as they strolled, leaving Bob at the door with an impish grin on his face."

Everybody made themselves at home, playing, singing, serving, joining in toasts to their happiness and punctuating the air with lusty shouts that transformed the suite into a veritable Mexican fiesta. They followed the couple down to the waiting taxi.

"Did you remember the ring?"

"Yes," said Bob, "but I don't have any Mexican money, only American, to pay the judge."

"I'll soften him up with a song," Connie promised.

At the courthouse there was a line with other couples waiting to be married, some carrying infants in their arms. Diapers were changed and small voices bawled while the judge administered the wedding oaths sometimes in English, sometimes in Spanish.

After they tied the knot, the couple alighted to a nearby Catholic church for a self-administered, special blessing, then returned to their hotel to celebrate. Essentially, marriage frightened Connie Haines: "It was what I dreamed of, but I did not want my dreams to turn into a nightmare."

Connie felt guilty because she had eloped, thinking that her friends and fans would be disappointed. Ten months later, in 1951, she repeated her vows in the church, making it official at Beverly Vista Community Church in Beverly Hills. It was a beautiful wedding. Dr. Louis H. Evans performed the ceremony. At the reception Gordon MacRae and Frankie Laine sang for the happy couple.

The formal wedding of Connie and Bob De Haven, Beverly Hills, CA, 1951.

"A very special friend of mine, Velma Romedy of Jacksonville, traveled 3000 miles to my wedding. It was part of a pact we made as kids to be at each other's wedding. I returned the favor a year later."

The honeymoon destination was Mexico City and Acapulco. Then it was back to work. The whirlwind resumed: performing at the Cocoanut Grove in Hollywood's Ambassador Hotel; the Copely Plaza in Boston, and the Waldorf-Astoria in New York, followed by an appearance on television's "Colgate Comedy Hour" with Eddie Cantor, appearances on

Milton Berle's TV show, Ed Sullivan's show, and shows with Perry Como and Jackie Gleason.

"I recorded for Coral Records new songs such as 'Pink Shampoo,' 'Maybe It's Because,' 'Que Será Será,' 'How It Lies,' and I re-recorded 'Old Man Mose is Dead.' Then there was a big benefit back home in Jacksonville."

It was a homecoming for Connie and her new husband, and a chance for him to get to know where and how she grew up and experience the warm family love in her beautiful Southern home. The benefit was a telethon to benefit cerebral palsy, staged in the George Washington Hotel auditorium. It was a twenty-four hour fun-fest that raised $ 75,000.

Back in California, the couple purchased a two-story colonial on Laurel Canyon Boulevard in Studio City.

"I fell in love with it instantly. Originally it was a farm house on what used to be the Hormel Ranch. Newspapers in the attic were dated in the 1890's and the house was once used as a United States Army Cavalry headquarters. With no bathrooms or garage, we had to build them immediately. We re-styled the entrance and added a circular driveway. We kept the gracious stairway and the original doors and door hardware. Bob performed all the work himself."

The house became transformed into a small Southern mansion, reminding Connie of Jacksonville, with pine-paneled walls, a brick faced fireplace with a broad mantel, and built-in bookshelves. It was a beautiful home for the newlyweds to enjoy for the rest of their lives.

"In December, 1953 I was asked by the presidential chaplain to go on a preaching mission to Korea, Johnston Island, and Hawaii. Bob came, too."

The tour was arranged by Air Force General Carpentier, chief of chaplains at the Pentagon, and Chaplain Mike Carriker was their escort. She was to sing hymns at air bases and hospitals. The minister was Dr. Louis Evans, who had married them and who was now a minister-at-large for the Presbyterian Churches of America. She shunned all offers to commercially entertain while in Honolulu, keeping herself inspired through Dr. Evans, who was named by *Life Magazine* as one of America's ten greatest religious leaders. They stayed at the Royal Hawaiian Hotel, where Bob decided to try surfing.

"I'm renting a board. Want to watch?"

"Wouldn't miss it for the world. Shall I begin praying now?"

"Pray now—that I don't meet a mermaid out there."

Bob did very well with natural body coordination. After two or three false starts, he was on his way, soon hanging on for as much as ten minutes.

"Admit it," he whispered to Connie. "I'm the greatest."

"I admit it."

De Haven had to return to work, flight testing at Hughes. Connie continued on with appearances at Hickam Field, Wheeler Air Force Base, Tripler Hospital, and other bases in the Pacific, enjoying the singing of hymns and carols to servicemen, free of commerciality, freed for spirituality. Then on to Korea. She returned to Bob De Haven on Christmas Day.

Connie repeated performances stateside for servicemen with Dr. Evans for many weeks. She sang inspirational songs like "He Wears a Pair of Silver Wings," "Heartaches," and "I'd Rather Have Jesus Than Anything."

"Dr. Evans would talk to the soldiers and airmen after services and my singing, conferring with them about their personal problems and the meaning of their acceptance of Christ in their lives."

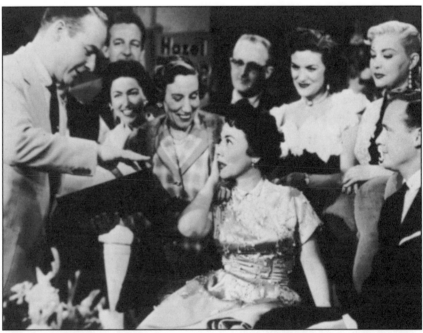

This Is Your Life, Connie Haines! *Above: Connie is the subject of Ralph Edwards' show. Enjoying her surprise: Harry James, Tommy Dorsey, Beryl Davis, Della Russell, Connie's mother, Doris Parnaby, Bob De Haven, 1954.*

"THIS IS YOUR LIFE, CONNIE HAINES"

In February, 1954, Connie was supposedly invited to take part in honoring Peter Potter, Beryl Davis' husband. "We want it to come as a surprise to him, Connie, so don't divulge the name to anyone. You understand," said Ralph.

"This Is Your Life" with Ralph Edwards was a nationally televised, prime-time show that honored public figures, entertainment and sports people. The subjects were usually unaware of being selected to be honored and were further surprised by a stream of visitors involved in their lives, past and present, actually appearing live on the show.

"But the shock came when Ralph handed me the big book that read *This Is Your Life, Connie Haines.*"

Connie's life story unfolded before millions of viewers. Edwards had a doctor standing by in case it overwhelmed Connie. The show covered Connie's life with appearances by her mother, sister, husband, Jane Russell, Harry James, Tommy Dorsey, Beryl Davis, Della Russell, and filmed segments with Frank Sinatra and Fred Allen. She cried through the entire show. Edwards presented clips from her movies, and the girls, Jane, Della, and Beryl, as well as Connie, sang "Do, Lord" from their Capitol album *The Magic of Believing.* At the time of the show "Do, Lord" was number fifteen on the charts. By the end of the following week it rose to number one.

"It's difficult to describe the feeling of having your life reviewed before your very eyes this way, much less before millions of people. I kept smiling for the cameras, but I was choked up and my eyes were wet throughout the show."

A year later, when Connie and Bob took a cruise aboard Henry Kaiser's *S.S. Leilani* to open his new Hawaiian Village, the "This Is Your Life" program became the subject of a two-page brochure announcing her appearance in the hotel.

"I fell madly in love with Hawaii and vowed I'd live there someday. The 'aloha-spirit' was very strong in those days." This was the time Connie was busily involved with once-a-week appearances on the "Frankie Laine Show," where they were known as *Mr. and Miss Rhythm.* The show was pre-recorded while they toured theaters all across the United States.

FRANKIE LAINE, 1999

"What a joy working with my wonderful and full of life pert Connie Haines. She is a great trooper and a very fine singer.

When we made the series of Guild Films together for television, I found out for myself how terrific she really was as a singer and friend. I can't bestow enough compliments upon her, and, more importantly, I consider her one of my best friends. We sang our hearts out together for several years. Like myself, she found the words of a song not just words, but true expressions of life by way of the feelings of the sincere poets of Tin Pan Alley who wrote them, expecting only the best interpretations. Connie Haines always delivered.

Connie continued her activities in the Hollywood Christian Group, enhancing Hollywood's image of its celebrities. The group's pillar of strength, Dale Evans, also once a Big Band singer with Anson Weeks, and her husband, Roy Rogers, sang religious numbers, just as Beryl Davis, Jane Russell, and Connie recorded similar material for Capitol.

"At our annual dinner, held in the Mayfair Room of the Wilshire Hotel, Ronald Reagan (before he was elected Governor of California) spoke after I sang: 'I prayed before each Saturday's game,' he recounted to our group, 'thinking I was the only one. But I found out that every one of the thirty-five varsity players did likewise. What's more I found that most of them, like me, did not pray for victory but more like...let me do my best, let the best team win, and let me have no regrets,' said the future Governor and President of the United States."

Present were Jane Russell and her husband Bob Waterfield; Irene Dunne; June Haver; Marie Wilson; Terry Moore; and the Gordon MacRaes; Colleen Townsend; Beryl Davis; Rhonda Fleming; Loretta Young; Ricardo Montalban; and scores of other entertainment industry members, all professing their faith.

"The early fifties were a turning point in my life, away from lucrative nightclub engagements and toward the more spiritual things of life. I still went on theater tours, cut records, taped radio shows, and made television appearances. But, oh, how I resisted the clinking glasses and smoky air of the nightclub, and especially the gambling clubs. This change had begun even before I was married to Bob and caused a few hairy moments between me and my manager, Bullets Durgom."

"Your reputation is bad, because it's *too* good," Bullets complained. "people want to hear about your being at this or that nightclub with so-and-so, not autographing Bibles for choir children at a church."

"Years later, I took Bullets, then my ex-manager, to a Monday night meeting of the Hollywood Christian Group. It was at Jane's house. Halfway through the evening, when I did not see Bullets, I figured he'd

checked out. But then I caught him sitting quietly on the floor completely absorbed in what was happening. Later he told me that it was one of
the best evenings of his life. At last Bullets was able to understand my
dedication, something that had baffled him for years."

Of course, there were many who noticed a contradiction in Connie's
image as a singing star and her ever-expanding church activities.
Broadway columnist Earl Wilson cornered her during a 1952 interview:

"You won't play gambling clubs?"

"No, I won't," Connie was firm.

"Why?"

"It's not that I'm trying to reform anyone. If they choose to gamble—
let them. I understand them. I still love them."

"What do you mean, 'you love them?'"

"I love everybody !"

"Do you love Jimmy Fidler ? "Fidler was a competitor columnist.
"Everybody."

"If you love the gambling public, why won't you sing for them ? "

"I feel I have a personal obligation to a lot of people, especially the
youth of our country. I try to be an example as much as I can. What must
they think of my singing in a gambling spot on Saturday night, which the
church teaches against, and singing in a church the next morning?"
Connie got firmer.

"How do you think it will affect your career ?"

"My career has zoomed up since I've been saying no to gambling
places."

"Your manager says it's in spite of that decision and rather due to his
expert managing."

"I say it's my faith."

"Connie, how old are you ?" Wilson took a new tack.

"You and your big pencil," she laughed, "You expect I'll tell a fib. Not
after all that talk about religion. I'm twenty-nine, going on thirty."

"Wilson printed the interview verbatim under the headline *See You in
Church*, closing with 'Shucks, I wish more glamour dolls would get religious. It would be so much easier for columnists to tell the truth about
them.'"

FEAR OF FLYING

During her days with Dorsey, the band was involved in a near plane
crash which frightened and therefore instilled a fear of flying into Connie.

For the next ten years she traveled the trains of American—the Santa Fe and the Super Chiefs. Now married to a test pilot, she made up her mind to get over the fear of flying. With help from Bob, she worked on it, eventually working her way back to flying in commercial planes. First, she took a trip to New Orleans with her mother. As luck would have it, the plane hit a storm and was pelted with hail. The plane was tossed about as though it were made of cardboard. People cried and prayed. They wailed and screamed. What a test for the neophyte. Her mother gave up flying for twenty years.

Seven years into their marriage, Bob and Connie decided to fly in his private plane and prove she had licked her fears for good. Their one-engine Bonanza took off for Mexico City along the ocean route. Flying between the shore and mountains was the safest route for a small plane, Bob, among the finest pilots, assured her.

"I would never have flown in such a plane if it were not my husband piloting. The small craft belonged on a charm bracelet, not on a runway. Our friends Nancy and Ashley Orr joined us. Ashley, an attorney, was executor of our wills and godfather to our son."

Bucking headwinds took more fuel that they had in the tanks. They had to prepare for an emergency landing. "I kept praying as Bob swore up and down, 'God, forgive him, he doesn't really mean it.'"

Bob radioed the Navy. There were cross winds as they put down, but they made it. Bob refueled and they took off again. Then he discovered he'd been given the wrong fuel—fuel too heavy for the plane. He had to jettison most of it, along with some baggage, in order to get over the mountains between there and Mexico City. Mission accomplished.

"I was now a fearless flier, and later I even took flying lessons. Being married to Bob practically put me in the cockpit with him. I didn't have to test-fly, but I most certainly had to share the pressures of that risky occupation with him. He needed lots of tenderness, attention, and love to assuage the stress of the test pilot's day. That's exactly what he received from me. I loved giving it, and he loved receiving it, and life together was good."

THE LITTLE ONES

KIM AND ROBERT

"How I wanted children! Surely I was not to be denied this birthright. Were the doctors who said during my childhood illness that I could not ever have children now to be proven right?"

For Connie, married life was incomplete without children. One day, finding herself in a Catholic church before a figure of Mary, she knelt to pray:

"Mother of Jesus, certainly you know how much I want a child of my own. You know the blessing of motherhood more than any mother. If you have any power, please pray that I may have a child."

Nine days later Connie Haines was pregnant. They would be trying days with husband Bob De Haven.

"It was a time when I could not give as much. Being pregnant and having to struggle to keep the child, especially when there was hemorrhaging, took attention away from Bob. He became irritable and nit-picky. One evening he was at me in the kitchen."

Bob was impatient, expecting dinner on time as usual, which became difficult for Connie. He taunted and needled her until she lost her cool.

"Bob! You stop it !" she was crying more every day. It appeared to be exactly what he wanted, haranguing her into a hysterical fit of crying, crying that she was afraid would injure the baby's chances of surviving the pregnancy. She was driven out of control.

"I felt myself hemorrhaging again. I screamed, 'If I lose my baby, I'll kill you!'" She collapsed in a heap on the floor. Bob had found the breaking point.

The doctor relegated Connie to bed. The bleeding subsided after a few weeks. Dr. Alfred Helfond had to spend more time with a pouting, immature Bob De Haven than with Connie, advising him to handle his wife with "kid gloves," and to be calm and gentle with her if he expected to become a father.

When Kimberly De Haven was born, Bob was thrilled.

"There could not have been a more tender, loving father and husband. I became pregnant again. Having two babies within a year does not exactly strengthen a woman's constitution. It crippled me for nearly three years."

Connie felt a magnificent feeling being a mother. After all those visits to specialists and clinics over a period of five years, her daughter became the reward, the answer to her prayers. At the time, she had her own television show and appeared on "CBS's Playhouse 90." One week the drama, the next week a fast-moving musical cavalcade with Jane Russell and Beryl Davis. She also was a guest on "Shower of Stars" with comedian Jack Benny.

Several months into her second pregnancy, Connie had to slow down the pace. "For the last show, Jane had to pick pregnant me up in her arms and prop me up on a stool. I had the doctor's okay to wear a waist cinch-

With children Robert De Haven, Jr. and Kim.

er. With that and a full skirt, I hid my secret from the audience. Lucky the cameraman didn't do too may close-ups."

Connie became completely immobile once Robert De Haven, Jr., was born. Here was a little one-hundred pound *Snootie Little Cutie* producing a big ten pound baby. Baby Bob had been acting like a brace within her body.

"Hey, Robert, did you know you *supported* your mother even before you were born ?"

Connie and Bob began building a new house in Bel Air. They stayed with Deedee and Nana Gray (Dick Gray's parents) in their Spanish Mission style home. Her post maternity care bedroom became a hospital room with a hospital bed in their friend's home. A brace around her hip held her together. A corset with braces up the back kept her spine straight. "The doctor declared I had a hormone imbalance due to pregnancy. They were not sure if I would ever walk again. When did I hear that before? They didn't know me—or about my faith in Jesus Christ."

The ligaments had softened. Connie had developed muscle atrophy.

She took her kids on tour. Roosevelt Hotel, New Orleans, 1954.

"I was just a bag of bones and a hank of hair," she would explain to visitors, as they watched her pull herself up into a sitting position with the aid of an overhead trapeze-like contraption.

With a nurse on regular duty and her mother attending her daily, she noticed Bob getting more and more tense by the day. Connie experienced no pain in either delivery, but it was a miracle that her loose bones did not pinch a nerve to cause extreme pain. All though the ordeal, Connie remained cheerful, positive and brave. She pulled herself up, hanging on to the steel bar to steady herself.

"Doctor Al, I know you understand when I tell you that I see myself performing again and taking care of my babies—and even expect to dance again.

"I feel that I'm surrounded by prophets of doom who seem to be working against me. I *will* return to my work. "

"They don't mean to work against you, Connie; they feel they are softening the blow for you. People tend to sell other people short. They don't have your great spirit, so they don't understand. You'll show them. You have inner strength."

"Thanks. See you tomorrow, Doctor Helfond."

Weeks became months, and Bob De Haven became irritable and even hostile. Connie's infirmity was added pressure for the fragile make up that was Bob De Haven. The two children, nurses around the clock, he just couldn't cope with it. Whenever he tested airplanes, he was risking his life. When he flew, he tested firing equipment to check the strain of the plane. He flew at shattering speeds. Home became a strain for him instead of a refuge.

Helen O'Connell and Connie's other dear friends took her place in contractual radio and television commitments. Fortunately, the Frankie Laine television series was pre-recorded. With a radio, television and telephone by her side, she was able to communicate to the house builder all necessary information regarding the problems of building and expediting.

"I was like a person who had polio and was paralyzed from the waist down. I was a better mother than a wife in that condition. It was a joy to have the babies in bed with me for a while each day."

It was eight months after birth that Connie was able to begin the reversal of the atrophy. She did all the work necessary to move first the toes, then the ankles, and finally the legs. Heavy weights were put on her legs, and she had to lift those weights. She did it. Then a wheelchair, then crutches.

Now she was able to accomplish simple chores in the kitchen and around the house. "I could not do all I wanted to do for Kim and Rob.

Kim was a toddler, and Rob, even though a year younger, walked first. To please Bob, I would push ahead, push too hard, and damage my body, finding myself back in bed."

Two years without a single public appearance did not affect the ratings. Being on television with Frankie Laine three times a week did the trick for the convalescing song star. Magazines kept up the interviews. Columnist kept her name in front of the public. Recordings were continually played on the air. *The Los Angeles Times* ran a feature with photos. Art Linkletter and his son came over to her house with remote control and did an entire show about Connie with the children, the ensuing invalid state, and her first faltering steps with the kids.

Four years had passed, four years in which Connie's love for Bible study grew and grew together with her love for the children, her husband, and for all those she knew and worked with. Her career returned beginning a new contract recording new spirituals with a new trio comprised of Jane Russell. Beryl Davis, and herself (Rhonda Fleming had just left the group). It was as if she never missed a beat.

For Connie it felt that: "Bob and I resumed where we left off. When you are carrying a man's child within you, nothing can ever equal the feeling, the love you then have for him, to know that you really have life within you that the two of you have created. That is really love."

However, Bob's interest in Connie had waned during her incapacitation. He had expected a wife to be a wife, not a cripple. He thought it existed only in her mind, although the doctors spent hours with him showing X-rays and explaining how it was not possible for Connie to walk with her spine twisted to one side and the pelvic area still open from childbirth. He could not understand or accept the facts. It was the beginning of the end for them. First, there was no letup between arguments. Their communication ceased. They grew apart.

"Our marriage was a sham, but in no way did we project to others our true situation. They saw diamond rings, mink jackets, and the convertible that Bob continued to lavish on me. He would create storybook Christmases, bestowing hundreds of gifts upon me. My family and friends saw this generous side of Bob. What they did not see was the torment to which I was subjected."

The arguments went on. Connie was back in bed with collapsed legs. The tension was unbearable. Bob drank. They became extreme opposites. Bob was able to magnify each difference. Connie confided in her friend Debbie Reynolds, who was going through her problems with Eddie Fisher, so they cried on each other's shoulder.

"The attacks by Bob grew worse. The attacks of physical incapacitation grew worse. An endocrinologist and a bone specialist said that, if matters got worse, I would reach a point where I would not be able to recover. I had developed stiff arthritic joints. I consulted with Debbie's attorney. I asked him to prepare divorce papers."

Connie had her mother move into the house. At first Bob De Haven sulked, then he fought, contesting the divorce. Bob locked the refrigerator, bugged the telephone, and performed other acts of resistance and domination. He also claimed to be sick. Nothing he did worked to restore their relationship. The court awarded custody of the children to Connie.

"Bob's final words to me were: 'It's not finished.' It wasn't."

The alimony and child support totaled seven hundred dollars a month. If she earned money, there was no alimony check. She gave up the alimony and went back to work.

"I decided to take the children to Jacksonville for an Easter (1962) vacation with my eight aunts and uncles. Bob's weekend attacks on me were troubling their young minds. I felt they needed the stabilizing influence of a Southern Christian experience, doting Christian aunts, uncles, and cousins."

During the first two years of the divorce, Bob De Haven never missed a Friday afternoon flying to Newport Beach from the private Hughes Aircraft field in Los Angeles, taking a taxi to the house, and whisking the kids off to a plane for a flight back to L.A., where he would keep them until Sunday night.

"Kim, seven years old, and Rob, six, would smother me with hugs and kisses when they left. But their return was a different story."

"Sometimes they were in tears, and sometimes they were simply silent."

"Mom, Dad said you really don't love me and Kim. He says you're just acting. You love us, don't you Mommy?"

Connie could not understand how a father could torture his own kids that way. She always encouraged them to love their father. In the two years following there had been eight separate "orders to show cause" subpoenas. Connie would tend to be nervous when the doorbell rang. Bob would not stop the legal harassments. Connie's attorney would call him to say the children would be away with her for this or that weekend.

"Oh, God, help me, I would think. It's a good thing my family surrounded us with total love. They showered the children with attention and affection. How could I bring the kids back to that California tug-of-war?"

Connie planned to purchase a house where a helicopter could not land. It was a one story colonial with lawn and gardens just off the Arlington River. She hired a maid whom she grew to adore and entered the kids in an Episcopal school—Grace Parish Day School. They adjusted quickly to their new life. Connie hired a new attorney, Arthur Gutman, who advised her to seek relief in the Florida courts which, through his remarkable efforts, granted her full custody of the children under Florida law. This would subject Bob De Haven to prosecution for kidnapping if he tried to take the children. His access to aircraft of all types has allowed him to take the law into his own hands in the past. De Haven was advised by the court accordingly.

Arthur Gutman was able to control De Haven and keep Connie constantly informed of matters while she was on tour. All she had to do was pick up a phone.

"I was at home with the children one Saturday when I saw Bob. The children were playing croquet. I had just been gazing out of the window when I saw a car slow up and drive on. I quickly called the kids into the house. Then I dialed Arthur. 'He's here.'"

"Keep the kids in the house. Leave the rest to me, "advised Gutman.

"There was some commotion outside—voices. Cars drove away. In a few minutes the phone rang."

"He's on the way back to the airport. He won't bother you."

Connie picked up her Bible. "I opened it to Romans 8:28: 'All things work together for good to those that love God and who are called according to his plan.'"

The day before Connie left for an engagement with Jane Russell and Beryl Davis, she called every member of the family to remind them to keep an eye out for Bob De Haven and to call Arthur if he showed up.

A guard was hired to transport the kids to and from school.

Immediately after a performance for President John Kennedy at the White House with songwriter Jimmy McHugh, who wrote "Sunnyside of the Street" and "Coming In On a Wing and a Prayer", Arthur Gutman called Connie at her hotel.

"He kidnapped the kids. But we grabbed him at the airport. The kids are fine. He is in jail. The hearing is tomorrow. Can you make it back?"

Arthur related the story at the airport upon Connie's arrival.

Bob had flown in to a private airstrip in Jacksonville and was driven by chauffeur to another rented car that he drove to the school where he presented the headmaster with a restraining order from a California court. The children were released, but her mother was notified. Having foreseen this, Arthur called police who came sirening into the air strip and cut it off nearby the waiting plane. Guns drawn, De Haven gave up, released the children, and was led away in handcuffs to the cries of the confused children. He had actually tried to take a gun from a policeman.

Faced with cries from the children, saying; "Mommy, you're not going to let them put my daddy in jail? "Connie relented. "How could I only sing of God's love and express anything less myself? What a terrible experience for my children—they never got over it."

Bob De Haven walked out of the hearing laughing—his sarcastic expression saying, "It's all in the game, Connie."

"Being married to Bob De Haven for some ten years was a valuable experience for me. I don't think, however, that I would do it all over again. However, it left me open and receptive to God's plan. He helped

Beryl Davis, Connie Haines and Jane Russell. Reach out to their audience.

76

my thinking capacity and taught me how to use it. It was wild and often hairy, but I grew from the lessons.

"It's impossible to recapture all the ups and downs now. I'm happy to have my children to show for the marriage. He was the only man in my life that I ever thought of marrying who eventually had children. God must have meant it to be."

Jane Russell had her own view of the De Haven affair. "The whole thing was pretty rough for Connie to weather. He was trying to fly back and forth and kidnap the kids. It was terrible for a while, but her faith got her through. It was unfortunate for the kids all the way around. Fighting over kids is ridiculous."

LES GIRLS

Beryl Davis, Connie's lifelong friend who is still performing today, and Jane Russell, one time band singer and prolific actress and personality, along with Connie Haines, prayed their way up the ladder.

"We became the Big Three," said Jane. "Our first record together was 'Do, Lord' for the Decca-Coral label."

"We recorded that song over and over," said Beryl, "Each time we thought we had it. But in this recording business it's not what you think, it's what the A&R (artist and repertoire director) thinks, and the engineer, and the sound man in the booth."

"Waiting for our turn in the studio, we heard that excited, 'That's it! That's it!'" recounted Connie, "But it never seemed to come for us."

"Pray with us," said Jane to the musicians.

"Who, me?" The drummer acted as if he were being singled out for an execution.

"Yes," said Jane, "All of you."

Jane's words were the command of a first sergeant. "It's pray time, fellows. Let's have a prayer."

The musicians came forward as the girls reached out their hands, guiding them into a circle.

"We three girls closed our eyes and bowed our heads..and the musicians followed suit," said Jane.

"I peeked and caught a few roaming eyes and winks," Beryl remembered.

"Dear God, let the love we have for You and for each other come though in our voices and in our music. Make us one, together. Amen." They stood for a moment, feeling the spirit of God. Then they let go of

Jane Russell, Connie and Beryl Davis, 1956.

the hands. "The boys held fast, not making a run for it as we girls had expected," said Jane. "But they stood there for a moment; it was not so bad after all."

Then they all went to work. "I had lost count of the takes when... 'That's it!' It was Bing Crosby, part owner of Decca at the time, who was usually never there. 'You gals have a hit...maybe a million seller. How about that!' Bing said with enthusiasm.

"Just to see Bing would have shaken up us girls, but to have him walk in and say we have a million record seller on our hands was really one of the thrills of my life," said Connie. His voice was enthusiastic and ever so familiar. Bing was right on target with his prediction.

"We girls always prayed before a rehearsal, before a show, before a recording," Jane continued, "We converted more powder rooms into holy ground that there were ever holy grounds before. We didn't care whether the musicians were Jewish, Buddhist, or Christian. If I said, 'Come on, boys, let's have a pray,' the musicians were pulled into the prayer circle."

Once, at the supperclub theater in the Riviera Hotel in Las Vegas, Connie had trouble with a zipper on her dress. Jane and Beryl finally got it unstuck, but, they used up their prayer time. They almost didn't make it to the stage on cue. After the show, several musicians collared the girls backstage.

"Don't ever do that to us again," moaned the drummer, Sidney Bulkin.

"We made the stage on time," Connie insisted.

"It wasn't that," chimed in Rocky Cole. "You didn't get here in time for us to pray. We couldn't perform out there. Did you hear how sad the horns were? We just couldn't get it all together."

"The whole band, it seemed, was uptight because there was no pray time," Jane figured.

It's funny, when you talk with Jane Russell or Beryl Davis today, they remember those incidents with loving kindness in voices that remain the same as they did back in the 1960s. Both have youth and joy in their voices and in their hearts.

Can you imagine three women living together, working together, starring together—and still loving one another? Here you have different upbringings, different personalities, different walks of life—Beryl, a big band singer from England, where her father was a bandleader and she a vocalist at a very young age, the last vocalist to sing with Major Glenn Miller in the Army Air Force Band in London, the night before he took that fateful flight in 1944; Jane Russell of Canadian parentage resettled in the American West, a lone gal in a family of four brothers, a wonderful, capable motion picture actress and one-time band singer with Kay Kyser's band; and Connie Haines, a Southern belle from the deep South and of French descent.

"We had our differences, our fights, and some tears, but one overriding similarity transcended our differences—we lived by the Scriptures. We never allowed the sun to go down on our anger," Beryl noted firmly.

"Every night we would go back to our suite lined up in a row. Both of the girls were married. I was divorced from Bob. But we had eight kids among us,"reminded Connie.

The girls frustrated the press. In a place like Las Vegas, the girls would remain in their room after a show. They had a refrigerator. "We had a bite to eat, talked, prayed, and then went to sleep," said Beryl. The press would have them painting the town, anyway, just to fill their papers.

For Connie, who could not tolerate cigarette smoke, Jane was her fireman: "Get out of here with that cigarette," Jane ordered, "Our lead trumpet can't sing." (Jane felt that Connie's pace- setting voice was like a lead trumpet.)

"Oh, she's just a hypochondriac," retorted one smoking visitor. "It's all in her mind."

"It's not in her mind, stupid; it's in her throat. We'd lose thousands of dollars a week—OUT!" Jane pointed to the door. Later, she fashioned a few "NO SMOKING" signs and would carry them to wherever the girls performed, posting them on doors and in other conspicuous places.

Jane was known to all as *Old Aunt Jane*. Some say she wanted to soft-sell her sexuality, because she certainly has retained her classically feminine beauty to this day.

The girls made some pretty good money with the success of the recordings. "My profit went to tithe," said Jane Russell, "because I made my money in pictures. I know Connie and Beryl also tithed, but they needed most of their money, because singers in those days didn't earn too much."

"When I was pregnant with my second child, in bed on doctor's orders, there'd be a whistle outside the window," said Connie.

"It's me. Old Aunt Jane is here."

"What do you want?" Connie would strain to say.

"I'm coming up to pray. We're going to have a good pray time."

A minute later, Jane Russell and her dear friend Connie Haines would be praying by the bed. Then Aunt Jane would put her arms underneath Connie, lift her up, and carry her down to her convertible and drive to her mother's house and private chapel in the Van Nuys area.

Jane's mother was a minister. Her father passed away at an early age, and this was his estate. The whole family lives there in separate houses and apartments: Jane's four younger brothers, their wives, and the twenty-one children. Jane explained: "I had four younger brothers, and they have all given my mother lots of grandchildren. Each boy had a house on a piece of property and my mom's house was in the middle. So I would go over there and it was always *Aunt Jane*. I began to sign letters and greeting cards *Old Aunt Jane*. That's how it really came about. Now, everybody calls me *Old Aunt Jane*."

"It's a beautiful compound," said Connie, "off Woodman Boulevard with a chapel in the center. Mother Russell is the 'Charismatic Leader.' Many think this means Pentecostal. Actually the Charismatic movement is in to Presbyterian, Methodist, and even Catholic groups. She is not Pentecostal. She is a nondenominational Christian Church, and she is a minister of the gospel of Jesus Christ. "

Now, at the time when Connie was pregnant with her second child, Jane's brothers would carry her down the stairs, past the beautiful waterfall and gardens to set her down in the chapel.

"The whole family would join in, led by Mother Russell. I would feel the love that flowed through those people."

Jane Russell, Beryl Davis, Rhonda Fleming and Connie Haines.

Connie had first met Jane and Beryl before she married Bob De Haven. Jane was married to Bob Waterfield, and Beryl had just married radio and TV personality Peter Potter.

"If the three of us had any serious squabbles, it was over billing: how our names would be listed. Not as you might think, however. Jane wanted hers last, but we made her first, and I was second—in the middle."

81

That had some musical validity, too, since Connie carried the melody and the girls provided the harmony. Jane sang bass and Beryl the equivalent of tenor harmony. When the girls first got together to practice in the basement of Beryl's St. Stephen Episcopal Church, Della Russell (vocalist Andy Russell's wife) and Jane Russell agreed to sing at a fund-raising event. Jane has just completed the movie *Gentlemen Prefer Blondes* with Marilyn Monroe.

"I suggested we sing 'Do, Lord,' an old church spiritual. Della balked at first, saying, 'I'm Catholic. We don't sing that song in our church.' Said Beryl, 'I'm from London. I never heard it either.'"

"Then Jane said, 'Well, you're going to learn one right now.' They picked up on it real fast. We sounded great and sang together for the first time that night for our church group."

"Connie and I knew all those spirituals," said Jane, "She was raised in the Baptist Church and I was raised in a non-denominational evangelical, so we taught the other two."

Excited, with voices blending perfectly, they were given a rousing ovation. Then things began to happen for them. In the audience was a man from Coral Records. Connie had sold him a ticket. Two weeks later they recorded "Do, Lord."

After Della Russell dropped from the group, Rhonda Fleming, a devout Mormon, joined with Beryl, Jane, and Connie. Harmonizing was new to Rhonda, who had always done solo work. But she fit right in with the others. They called themselves Four Girls and were soon recognized as the most beauteous quartet of hymn singers ever assembled. Somehow, even with other commitments, they managed to keep going.

"We did Abbott & Costello's 'Colgate Comedy Hour' on Easter Sunday and a number of guest appearances on other shows. 'Do, Lord' was going great guns, but that's not all. We received invitations from every corner of the entertainment world. We sang 'Do, Lord' on Hedda Hopper's radio show for Easter Seals, on Bob Hope's show, Red Skelton's, Ed Sullivan's, the Milton Berle Show, Arthur Murray's program, and Gary Crosby's first show…and you name it…we were on it."

When the girls were interviewed, it was "Bosoms and Bibles, "a phrase the press hung on them. "We shed a few tears over it," said Jane, "But, we might as well have a sense of humor about this and just hope that they spell our names right."

Some religious leaders frowned upon the enthusiasm and joy the girls put in what they considered to be solemn hymns. Jane's reply to this one was: "Real church people don't have an awesome fear of God. Rather, it's

Les girls Jane Russell, Connie, and Beryl Davis with Red Skelton, 1965.

a warm, loving feeling for Him. Our songs are joyful and happy." Jane was a great spokesman for the girls.

After three years as a quartet, Rhonda Fleming quit the group in 1957, reducing it to a trio. She was burdened with movie commitments. Beryl, Jane, and Connie decided to carry on. The three were contraltos, but Beryl moved from the alto spot to the tenor harmony and Jane sang bass. Connie remained the lead voice. They added some popular songs with a positive message to their repertoire, but kept on giving the bulk of their earnings to churches and charities.

The girls became the decade's leading pop gospel singers. They were the first to record spirituals on pop labels and launch the gospel trend of the time. They made twenty-four hit records with both Capitol and Decca Records.

They individually continued their own careers. Beryl had started hers off as a singing star in England at the age of fourteen. At sixteen she sang at a party honoring Queen Elizabeth on her sixteenth birthday. After singing with Major Glenn Miller's Army Air Force Band, she was brought through a radio contract to the United States to sing with Frank Sinatra on the "Your Hit Parade" radio show. Beryl always handled the election of designs for the girls' clothes and her esthetic taste provided just the right missing links in some of the musical arrangements.

Jane's sensual oriented film career, with features such as *French Line, The Outlaw, Gentlemen Prefer Blondes, Paleface,* with Bob Hope, and other shows had censors wearing out their scissors. Jane was earning very good money from a twenty-year contract with Howard Hughes. She also kept busy with an orphanage adoption organization which she founded (WAIF) with the royalties of "Do, Lord. "

"Jane's background in films helped her help us with lighting. She carried her own gelatins with her to transform into correct coloring some of the harsh and purple spotlights. She sparred with the press beautifully,

Louis Armstrong cuts the cake in honor of his 50 years in show business with Connie, Beryl, and Jane present.

blocking their sex-oriented questions good-humoredly and bringing the interviews into spiritual focus."

When a reporter asked Jane "What do you do, Jane?" she would usually reply, "Absolutely nothing, if possible." That was Old Aunt Jane.

"Of course," said Connie, "I had my marriage, my children, my illness, my divorce."

In Rhonda Fleming, who stayed with the group for a short time, they had a singer who was a trained mezzo-soprano. What a job for her to phrase in the gospel vein and swing. For instance, in "Do, Lord" Rhonda's cultured voice gave it the operatic *Lor-r-r-d*, rolling her *r's*, while Connie and Jane sang it in the Southern *Lawd*.

No matter what the three were doing or where they went, when the need arose, they found a way to get together and sing for a cause.

The girl's manager, Sam Lutz, understood them. Other agents, producers, and cameramen in show business tried to change them, pressuring them to get the spiritual dimensions out and the sex dimensions in. The girls would not compromise. They were taking less money as a group than they could earn individually because they had a calling. There was no other reason for them to be performing together.

"We were children of God, working together in Oneness."

However, the girls gave in to sing in Las Vegas, but would not shrink from their vows. They did pop tunes, but with a spiritual message, like Ervin Drake's "I Believe," Johnny Mercer's "Accentuate the Positive," or Jimmy McHugh's "Sunny Side of the Street."

"My marriage caused no problems for the trio. Neither did the birth of my first baby. Just a few months of interruption. The second pregnancy crippled our career, and the trio came to a halt. We did not give in without a fight, and we went down singing. How can you disappoint Jack Benny, host of 'Shower of Stars'? It took place in my fifth month."

Jane and Beryl made a seat for Connie to leave the dressing room. She had crutches, but they just made a seat locking hands together. They carried her to the stage and sat her—in a bouffant skirt—on a very high stool.

That night, before the Benny show, Jane found out that a third baby she had applied for adoption of was *born*. "I've just had a baby"! she cried. Little Buckey was born as Connie was five months with Robert.

"My pregnancy and Jane's telephone call set Beryl on a weeping jag. She wanted another child. So, instead of praying for the show that night, we prayed for Beryl to have another baby.

Beryl actually conceived that night and named the baby Melinda. Connie's son Robert had a crush on Melinda since he was a small boy and hoped one day to marry her.

RESUMING A CAREER

In 1959, Connie Haines' career resumed. Some of her friends were worried. "Go back to Las Vegas," they advised. She had heard those words many, many times. She literally let it bounce off her. Stories about her *mystery ailment* pervaded and captivated the media. The headlines read: **Connie Haines Bounces Back With Aid of Faith or Vocalist Thanks God For Recovery From Mystery Ailment.**

"It all began when Beryl and I decided to go to the Brown Derby in Hollywood. It was my favorite place for lunch. It was really my first time back in circulation. The walls of that famous restaurant were covered with photos of all the famous movie stars. I was honestly amazed to find my own photo among them. Telephones there were installed at every table. We sat in the booth across the booth from Clark Gable and Ava Gardner. For a young entertainer like myself, it was always so exciting. We were star struck, as always.

"Bob Thomas, the columnist, was there and came over to see what all the current commotion was about concerning those headlines. He became interested in a comeback story, and in a few days it appeared in his nationally syndicated column, which touched off publicity follow-ups."

For Connie Haines it was dance appearances, horse shows, and a new recording contract with Dot Records. A popular Sunday TV show, "Faith of Our Children," signed her for thirteen weeks, replacing film dancer Eleanor Powell. Composer, orchestra leader Meredith Willson, who later wrote *The Music Man*, composed a special theme song for her entitled "Faith of Our Children."

"I wanted a comeback, but not in the standard Hollywood fashion. I wanted it to be more like a girl-next-door image. You have to have faith in faith. Then faith is rewarded."

Connie felt that, although she had nothing against money, God was the source of her supply. The girls had donated portions of the profits from "Do, Lord" and other recordings to their churches. She firmly believed in supporting religious activities wherever and whenever she performed. Hollywood columnist Louella Parsons wrote a story about her: "Contrast this courageous singer's story with that of some of the other denizens of the Hollywood jungle—the grasping, the mean, the small of soul—and you get the heartening feeling that perhaps after all it is faith, and not money, that is everything." Walter Winchell, the *New York Daily Mirror* columnist, followed up on a story about Connie's recovery and re-entry into performing again.

Within a year it was like old times for Connie Haines, with more singing opportunities that she could comfortably manage.

Accepting an appointment as musical entertainment provider for the Newporter Inn in Newport Beach, California, a multi-million resort hotel, for no pay, Connie was able to barter her efforts for a paid-up apartment; so it was like working "at home" with her children. Jane and Beryl helped her launch her shows with a Palm Sunday program of religious songs in the Inn's Empire Room. This allowed Connie to keep receiving her seven-hundred dollars a month child support for Kim and Rob, plus alimony from Bob De Haven, which collectively was not really enough to subsist upon .

"I booked the best acts: Russ Morgan and his Orchestra, the Mitchell Boys Choir, the beautiful King Sisters, maestro Les Brown and the Band of Renown, Freddy Martin and Dick Stabile and their orchestras. My job was to keep the place alive with big name entertainers for dining and dancing in this magnificent inn."

The children and Connie were very happy in this temporary situation. The kids enjoyed school, and Connie was able to spend a lot of time with them. But, even though she received the help from De Haven, she could not effectively manage financially, so she began singing once again with the girls.

"Even when I sang in church Bob De Haven would try to take away my financial support. My attorney would have to fight for my money. It was a losing game. I didn't want to leave the children behind so I decided to take them with me—nurses, tutors, and all."

Within two months she elevated her earnings to $25,000 a week with the girls, and up to $7,500 per personal television appearance. It was a successful year financially.

For four tremendous weeks the girls sang in Las Vegas at the Riviera Hotel with the great Louis Armstrong, who was celebrating his fiftieth year in show business. Pianist Billy Kyle, drummer Danny Barcelona, trombonist Trummy Young, all accompanied Louis, his familiar raspy pipes and lyric non-orthodoxy vocalizing his theme, "Sleepy Time Down South," and "Blueberry Hill."

Bob Hope came to see the girls perform and promptly invited them to appear on his Chrysler "Special" television show, which led to an appear-

With President Lyndon Johnson in the White House, 1964.

ance on Ed Sullivan's show and an engagement at New York's extravagant Copacabana.

"We really packed them in at the Copa. Manager Jules Podell was delighted. He was worried about the religious stuff. We were not only spiritual, but we were upbeat, optimistic, hopeful, glamorous, and positive. Who can resist that combination."

The entertainment weekly *Variety* reported favorably: "A trio of comely *femmes* with vocal chords to match."

By 1964, the girls were off again on more tours highlighted by an appearance at Miami Beach's Fontainebleau Hotel. Then two weeks at Chicago's Palmer House; a one-nighter for a GOP fundraiser in Albuquerque; the great annual Pin Oak Horse Show in Houston, Texas; the Kansas City Shriners show; the Casino Royale Club in Washington;

and back in Las Vegas for six weeks at the Riviera with one of Connie's favorites, George Burns.

While in Washington, the girls squeezed in an appearance at the White House Press Photographers Association dinner and a "Command Performance" for President and Mrs. Johnson at the White House.

"It's amazing. How do such things happen. Does your press agent work it out? Do you have to know the right people? All I can say that it came out of the blue four times for me: Presidents Eisenhower, Kennedy, Johnson, and Reagan. It was always a high-priority phone call at home from a secretary or representative ."

Connie enjoyed President Johnson the most. He guided Connie, Bob Hope, Jane Russell, Beryl Davis, and Leslie Uggams on a personal tour of the White House and surrounding grounds.

"He knew my children's godfather in Texas and inquired about him. I'll always remember how he'd pause at every door and say, 'Wait here.' Then he'd go in and turn on the lights. When we left each room he'd linger and turn off the lights, to the chagrin of the Secret Service agents who accompanied us. He was proud of his modest beginnings. Pointing to a photo of his Texas home where he was born, he said: 'Some difference, Connie. You could fit that entire home in one single room here in the White House.'

"He was a beautiful, sweet, down-to-earth man. When we went into the kitchen, there was Mrs. Johnson cooking one of his favorite dishes. He called out to his daughter to come over to meet us."

"No, Daddy," she called, "I can't. I have my hair in curlers." They all chuckled.

After the performance, tea was served. Throwing a wink at Bob Hope, Connie pretended she was going to hide the teacup under her mink stole for a souvenir.

"Mr. President!" Bob turned to him, "Watch the gal on your right. She has an eye on the furniture."

The President handed Connie a cigarette lighter with the inscription *Vice President*. Because of those historical events, he had taken office so suddenly he had little opportunity to acquire new lighters. "There's some *vice* left in me yet," he quipped.

In 1964 Jane Russell underwent an operation, which kept her out of the act. Connie moved back to Jacksonville, deciding that she had better build a new act. But, what kind?

"There'd be my Dorsey dependables, the blues numbers, and, of course, the spirituals. Still, there needed to be an updating. What else...but rock and roll."

Connie dug in. At first it was difficult for her to hear the rhythm patterns. They were different from everything she had done. She attended go-go places to learn the different dances: the Monkey, the Frug, and the Watusi.

"Oh, my aching back and my aching spine."

On the road with her new show, Connie, with advance publicity, sought out girls in each town to perform the spine-twisting, pelvis-pushing dances as she sang. It went over well. She caught on and was invited to record for Motown Records. As one reviewer commented: "Connie Haines lights a fire to her voice. It sizzles through about six bars, then whooshes ceiling-ward and, striking its apex, showers the room with multicolored sounds."

Ironically, Connie had made the first recording of "For Once in My Life" which was never released.

Beyond her divorce from Bob De Haven, Connie strongly feared another marriage, her relationships always trailing off from, first, exciting, fun-filled days and nights to eventual breakups, whether due to her fears or disparities between her and her suitors.

THE UNFORTUNATE RETURN OF BOB DE HAVEN

Through the years Connie had often received critical phone calls from Bob De Haven through his attorney concerning the children, followed by letters detailing his complaints, but never complimenting her for her efforts.

The Court ruled to send the kids to visit him. After the kidnapping, his attitude mellowed. She put Robert and Kim on the plane in Florida, during extended school holidays and summer vacations, and he met them in California.

"The visits made Bob happy, but it seemed to put an emotional strain on the children. They cried when they left and were in tears on their return. Divorce is hard on children—and they truly loved their dad. I fostered that in the kids. When he called one week to talk to them and I answered the phone, he asked to talk to me. I was in a state of shock. Bob had refused to speak to me since the divorce, only through attorneys. This was a very difficult way to raise children. 'Do you think we could work things out between us, Connie?' Bob asked sincerely.

"'I just wish it could be so, Bob,' I told him. 'You should have seen the way the kids arrived yesterday. They are being torn apart, and it hurts me.'"

"We were torn apart, too."

"Oh, Bob, it doesn't help to talk about that."

"You do remember, don't you, Connie."

"Of course."

"How do you get over your first love? I believe when you love someone, that never changes. It will be different, now. I am your husband, the father of your children, and they are an unbreakable bond between us. It's worth trying again for Kim and Bob."

"I thought then about how Bob had followed me all over the country to build up evidence that I was an unfit mother. He paid for detectives to follow me. I thought about the subpoena he had someone hand to me, and then rough me up in Las Vegas in an attempt to get me across the state line into California. I was saved by Beryl and Jane, who beat the guy off with her handbag. I had almost forgotten about the "cloak-and-dagger" tactics that he orchestrated so that I was afraid to go out on a date because he might rig some kind of a frame-up and build a case on it against me; about how he swore that he would never allow me to take the children because he said I was unfit, and how he maneuvered to get so many court orders that it would be impossible for me to heed them all and then to have me found in contempt. "

Connie recalled all those negative feelings. And in place of those forgotten memories came expectations. She found herself thinking about restoration of her marriage. Maybe a happy home. Maybe, she thought, this is what she needed. She knew she was still in love with Bob De Haven. She took the plunge once again to go back to him. Taking clothing and some belongings, the rest placed in storage, Connie closed the house and took her children to the plane and onward to California and, once again, with some reservations, to Bob De Haven.

"Bob met us at the airport. I searched his face for a flickering of love. I watched his arms for a sign of an impending embrace. None came. He looked straight through me."

He found them an apartment and drove them to it, hardly talking to Connie or the children. "I'll be in touch tomorrow," he said, closing the door.

"I watched out of the window as he drove away. I wept openly before the children as I fell into an exhausted sleep."

Two days later Connie was served with a summons to appear in court. Yes, it was the same Bob De Haven who harassed her after the divorce, who tried to kidnap the children in Florida, and who had her followed. This time he was suing for custody of Robert and Kimberly.

"My son, Robert, hero-worshipped his father, and I made a point of never destroying that. I did not need to get even with Bob. I had been sorely hurt and the children had suffered, but I wanted them to keep loving their father, and I worked overtime at accomplishing that. Mother thought I was going overboard: 'Connie, you know if you continue to paint this man as such a fantastic person, you're going to lose your kids.'"

Now, Robert wanted to live with his father. Her mother's observations were right. In his mother's arms, nine year old Robert didn't say much. But, then he'd say, "Don't make me love you, Mom, don't make me love you any more. I'm *not* going to love you."

Connie consulted her old friend Del Courtney before the court hearing. Del was very helpful in sustaining her courage during what has turned out to be some of the most difficult days of her life.

"I decided not to subject Robert to a court hearing, and allowed him to go with his dad, as he so-wished. I wanted no trial, no judge, no pain, for him or myself. I called my attorney and drew the appropriate papers assigning custody of our son to Bob De Haven. The court date was on a Monday, and Bob De Haven married a woman named Dianne on the previous day."

De Haven was shocked and amazed at Connie's unwillingness to fight him in court. She cried for what seemed like weeks and weeks. She sang publicly and cried privately until she could no longer sing a note.

"Nothing again could hurt me so much. It still hurts today. The cost has been high for us both, mother and son, although Robert finally came to understand how much I loved him.

LIFE WITH DEL COURTNEY

Del Courtney was a musician who began his career at the Claremont Hotel in Berkeley, California, in 1933. The band's longest engagement was at the Blackhawk Restaurant in Chicago for thirty-two weeks. The band was ideally styled for hotels, with a billing entitled "The Old Smoothie," and it played engagements at the New Yorker and Ambassador in New York, the Edgewater and Stevens in Chicago, the Roosevelt in New Orleans, the Baker and Adolphus in Dallas, the Royal Hawaiian in Honolulu, and the Ambassador's Cocoanut Grove in Los Angeles. Del headlined a television show in San Francisco for Sylvania, became a popular disc

jockey on radio station KSFO, and was a regular member of the "King Sisters Family Television Show" in the mid-sixties.

Del Courtney and Connie had been dating of sorts for about a year before the recent problem with Bob De Haven. It was a romantic relationship but somehow she had never felt the road was clear for her to think seriously about marriage.

"Sometimes, when one is hurt, when emotions are just below the surface, a word of kindness is intensified and more meaningful. It can be interpreted as even the deepest love. Now I thought I was in love with Del. I was free of the motive that could have been deceiving me—to have him as a father for my children, which, I must admit, had on occasion entered my mind.

"But now here I was with Kim, but without Robert."

Connie drew closer to Del Courtney. He seemed like a fine man. She admired him greatly. But, he was a very jealous man. Insanely jealous. It became public knowledge when he married Vonnie King, one of the singing King sisters, that their divorce was due to jealousy related problems.

Connie was ready, she thought, for someone to be possessive of her love. Courtney wanted a woman in whom he could have faith and who loved only him and wanted to do only for him. He wanted to be first and only.

"I felt I was such a woman. My career was something I never really needed. I wanted to retire completely to be a wife and mother. He would be good to Kim, and to Robert upon visits; he had proved himself on that score. A good husband is, Lord knows, what I sought and needed.

"Jane and Beryl lent me their ears, their shoulders, and their loving support during those days. I wanted to marry Del. But I had to be sure."

Del passed each test Connie threw in his path. Tolerant and understanding of her career, with a strong spiritual side, he passed test after test.

Connie invited her attorney, Arthur Gutman, to meet and evaluate Courtney. He caught the last show at the Riviera and sat with him for the entire show. The next morning Arthur called Connie to report favorable praises of Courtney. Del had passed his final exam.

"Del had to go to San Francisco. When he left Las Vegas, I sort of committed myself to him. We girls were appearing at the Tropicana. We arranged to be married in Las Vegas on my closing night, even though Del would have preferred a large California wedding."

With Jane and Beryl as matrons of honor, Delmore Anthony Courtney became married to Yvonne Marie Antoinette JaMais by a minister in a

At home with Del Courtney in happier days.

Las Vegas chapel in a perfect ceremony. She wore a gorgeous pink lace dress with a *mantilla* lace cap. Moments later, they drove back to the Tropicana and performed their show. To Connie, it seemed like the last performance of her life.

As the show ended, Del climbed to the stage, picked up Connie in front of a standing, applauding, and weeping audience and carried her off, later joining a party at the hotel. The girls' manager, Sam Lutz, arranged a fabulous reception for the couple. Well-wishers included her ex-boss Harry James, bandleader Lawrence Welk, newspaper columnist Earl Wilson, film actress Virginia Mayo, comedians Marty Allen and Steve Rossi, and her good friends, Jane Russell, Beryl Davis, and Rhonda Fleming.

"Our marriage was blessed in the Catholic Church the following Easter. It took place in the beautiful San Damiano Retreat House high in the mountains."

Connie had gone into Catholicism actively around 1960, about six years before the Courtney marriage. She was baptized a Catholic, because her father was, but was raised as a Protestant. Courtney was previously married in the Catholic church, so neither he or his ex-wife could be married to anyone else in the Catholic church, without special dispensation from the Pope in Rome. After application and months of waiting, the Courtneys finally got it cleared.

"I moved into Del's home on the outskirts of Oakland, in Orinda, California. It was a beautiful place. His mother, whom he had been close to all of his life, lived in a separate cottage. She was in her eighties at the time, a brilliant, sharp, beautiful woman."

Del kept his promises. He was good to Kim, great with Robert, and wonderful to Connie; "No more career. I'm taking care of you, Connie Courtney." That's what she wanted to hear. Jane and Beryl fulfilled the European contracts without Connie. She even permitted Del to handle the children's discipline. He was a great help to the kids, but she never realized how they resented his taking over.

"Del came first. He was that kind of man. He had been married twice before. But his mother came first, so we never had any privacy. Even when she was not present, Del obviously had her in mind. No wife could compete with this magnificently strong person. She was always there"

Another problem for Connie was Del Courtney's uncertain health. He apparently suffered many health and emotional problems for years, unbeknown to Connie. He was always filled with anxiety that he might become ill. This, Connie later determined, was why he needed a wife completely devoted to him.

The ultimate problem was the needless jealousy. Del imagined male competition as vividly as he did impending illness: "It's about time. I thought something had happened to you," he would say upon her return from a few hours at the beauty shop. "How long does the beauty parlor take? What happened to the rest of the time?"

"It was no use. It was never any use. No matter what proof I offered, once he decided to be jealous of some invisible competitor, he would express his disapproval and then clam up. Nothing I said, reminded, or asked would evoke a reply from him—not even a shrug. Just silence."

When he dished out the silent treatment, it was as if Connie were not present. Then, he would thaw as suddenly as he froze, and they would be man and wife again. Those were the exceptional days of their marriage.

The land Del Courtney's estate was built upon consisted of three and a half acres of rolling hills outside of Oakland, California. His father had willed it as part of a larger estate that was sold upon his death.

"We had some lovely moments in that home—coffee time in a bedroom suite, tea time on the verandah, champagne on the lower-deck lanai. It was cool and beautiful in Orinda even on the hottest summer day. A huge swimming pool was there when you felt like having a swim. There were four bedrooms in the house. The master bedroom was even larger than the living room. In the bedroom was a great marble sunken tub, exactly like an old Roman bath. I could gaze out a large window overlooking the garden, lavish stone birdbaths, and a unique statue of St. Anthony. "

When Connie married Del Courtney, she moved all the antique early American furniture that she had collected during her life into Orinda. Kim's two upper bedrooms were really a suite, with a sitting room and library with paneled walls and exquisite, detailed mouldings adorning the perimeters and doors. The events that happened in that room one day would play a key role in Connie's moving out of that beautiful house, a house that eventually became a house in turmoil, her marriage to Del Courtney dissolving into ashes.

"Del, I'm just finishing lunch with Jane. I'll be getting in the car in a few minutes."

"Del, I'm just getting under the dryer. I'll be through here in about half-an-hour."

"Del, I'm just getting on the freeway. I'll see you in a little while."

To build Del's trust, Connie would check in regularly by phone whenever she was away from the house, hoping that he would eventually realize there was no reason for jealousy. When she returned from a few days in LA with her mother, Connie, who had gone there for some breathing space and to clear her mind, drove straight to Trader Vic's restaurant to meet with Del.

"It was good to see Del, a man I loved. I understood his reactions. It was difficult for him to trust a woman. I tried hard. His style. His smile. This was the side of Del that made up for that other side. I so much wanted to make this marriage work. "

Del ordered Connie a *mai tai* cocktail, but declined anything for himself, complaining about his ailments: "…my hands are so numb. The bottoms of my feet feel funny. At the office today, twice my legs buckled from under me. The soles of my feet are dead, absolutely dead. Are my hands cold, honey?"

Connie felt his warm and moist hands. She thought Del's imagination was overactive. In the past, his medical checkups usually put his bodily concerns to rest, the symptoms often disappearing. They had a light dinner, chatted, and communicated beautifully that evening. Then, one of the Oakland Raider's owners sat down at the next table with his wife. They all greeted one another, when Del, after listening to Connie chat with them, suddenly said, "Quit talking!"

She quit talking.

"Come on, we have to go," Del said.

Del stood up, but his legs seemed to be collapsing under him. He fell to his knees. Connie screamed. Del's large frame now lay lifeless on the floor. Freddie, the restaurant manager, came running, as did the hostess and some friends. They lifted him up and carried him to his car. They raced towards the hospital, but Del protested, demanding they take him home.

A call to the doctor from Del confirmed that he seemed to have Guillain-Barre' syndrome. The doctor had examined him earlier that day with suspicions. This time Connie rushed Del to the hospital. The doctor met them there. Connie drove Del herself because he refused an ambulance.

She had assisted him down the stairs. He held on to the banister. She struggled to help him into the car and drove to the hospital . A spinal tap was taken. It was Guillain-Barre' syndrome. Connie did not realize the extent of the horror of that disease.

"I prayed hard that night. At the hospital the next day, the doctor hit me with the truth."

"I'll level with you," the doctor told her, "This disease is usually fatal to a man of Del's age. But, with courage, he'll have a fighting chance."

"What is that? How did he get it?"

"It's a virus. At least, that's what they think. It strips away the sheath around the nerves, like the insulation around wires. Then the nerves don't work. Right now it's a race against time. The nerves that trigger the lung muscles can be affected next."

In intensive care, six doctors were working on him. The illness could be fatal at any moment. A priest followed to administer last rites. Connie summoned Del's mother to his side. The three stood over him, watching.

He was scarcely breathing. The sacred ritual of last rites began, and Del seemed to relax into what Connie described as "the loving, saving arms of God."

Del was wheeled into surgery for a tracheotomy, where a windpipe was inserted into his throat, then connected to a respirator. They advised Connie to go home and rest. There was nothing she could do.

"Everything was going to be all right. I didn't feel as grim as the doctor. I sat with him. He lay there, comatose. Not a muscle twitched. Not an eyelid flickered. My heart ached with love and sympathy."

She went home to her young son, Bob, and daughter, Kim. Bob was back living with her again. "I explained to them that I would have to be at the hospital and they would have to take care of themselves. "Del's mother was also present to help them.

"We haven't had a case of this syndrome in years," the doctor admitted, "so we are guessing. At worst, Del could live a few hours or days. At best, he could pull through. But, in any case, there will be months of tough going."

He was so inert—so still.

"Yes, the nerves of his body are paralyzed. But he is conscious and very much alive, though unable to move."

Del came close to death several times that week. When intensive care alarms rang, Connie rose quickly each time, shouting for help.

He had been stricken on December 9th, being first treated for strep throat by his family physician. A robust Irishman; a music major at the University of California and St. Mary's; a successful bandleader during the 1940s; and since 1960, administrative director for the Oakland Raiders Football franchise, and also the current conductor of his own band, Del had seen the doctor the very day he collapsed.

The crisis continued for a while. In the room stood a readied maze of equipment designed to save his life.

On Christmas Day, Del experienced a fit of violent shaking.

"Ordinarily, this would be frightening, but, when you see a man shaking after lying motionless all those days, it's almost a welcome sign."

With tinted goggles put in place by an ophthalmologist to preserve eye moisture, Del Courtney resembled a character right out of *Buck Rogers*. It required three additional weeks for Del to first move his eyelids, to the delight and relief of his doctors, nurses, and an emotionally exhausted wife.

Four months later, Del Courtney remained in intensive care, unable to sit up. He had to learn to talk again. He remembered little of the ordeal. The cost to them exceeded $65,000.00, and months of physiotherapy lay ahead.

"You're going to do it, Del. You're going to be fine."

"I'm…gonna lick it…Connie."

By February he was speaking normally. Every day he gained more strength. Pulling himself up on parallel bars, using crutches, and climbing stairs, Del Courtney began an earnest recovery.

Connie had to handle the financial affairs of Del's estate, including all the bookkeeping. She became the conservator, bonded by the courts, in order for her to pay the bills. All previously purchased Christmas presents were returned to the stores. She protected all available capital, and gradually realized she was married to a wealthy man; still she tried to be responsible and conservative in handling his financial affairs. (This later challenged in court by Del himself with Connie was unequivocally cleared.)

At home everyone worried because of the unaccountability of Del's irrationality during convalescence. He walked the floors at night. Del had problems with his male nurse, George. With Del ill, and George with personality problems and an unrealistic view of Del's illness, serious problems existed between himself and Del. There were constant arguments and accusations of all kinds involving money and the safety of family members, even involving the children. George was dismissed, leaving his own set of scars on Connie. It was a chaotic time for the entire family. Del eventually recovered.

Connie reflected, thinking how she was blessed: "The many faces of love that God has created acquired one more to add to its numbers—one that was simultaneously feeling, frenetic, and fearsome."

Following the fearful and trying ordeal of Del's illness that Connie and her family had endured over many months, a final blow, in the form of outlandish, humiliating accusations against Connie by Del Courtney's attorneys, surfaced.

Served with court papers, stripped of her car and accounts at stores, Connie had to actually defend accusations in court. Del, through his lawyers, stated that she had misused his money and confiscated his jewelry. He didn't remember granting Connie a conservatorship while he was incapacitated. The case was eventually thrown out of court. Del's lawyers had put him through unnecessary court actions, even though it was obvious he was still in no condition to manage things himself.

A RAY OF LIGHT

On July 23rd, 1972, in Oakland, California, Kimberly De Haven and Alex Gomez were married. Kim was but seventeen.

"Because of their age, I had to be interviewed by a priest, and then Alex's parents had to do the same. Then we had to follow the same procedure before a judge."

"If there is any problem with the judge, and he won't sign the papers, have him call me. These kids are more ready for marriage than some thirty-year-olds," said the priest.

Because of the ordeal of Del's illness suffered by the family and the then current court scene, there was no one to give Kim away. Her father did not approve of the marriage because she was so young. So, sixteen-year-old Robert performed the honors for his seventeen-year-old Kim. Kim wore the wedding dress Connie had worn over twenty years before. There was not a dry eye in the church when young Robert marched his sister Kimberly down the aisle.

"Kim had wanted me to sing."

"You will, won't you, mother?"

"Kim, I won't be able to . I can't sing and sob at the same time."

"But, mother..."

"All right, but I'm warning you. I may have to ask Jane or Beryl to take over for me."

When the moment arrived, Kim faced her mother and said, "Stop crying, mother; you are going to sing 'Dream the Impossible Dream' for Alex and me. "

It was a traditional wedding. That's what Kim always desired, except that, after their vows, they turned to each other and sang the stirring Leonard Bernstein melody from *West Side Story*, "One Love."

"The wedding reception was out of this world. Ramon and Adona Gomez are the most loving, adorable people I've ever known, and I am so grateful my daughter married into such a loving family. At the time they owned an elegant Mexican restaurant in Lafayette, near Oakland, where the reception was held.

Flamenco dancers, a fountain of champagne, a three-tiered cake, and a mariachi band all contributed grandly to the affair. Robert had a rock and roll band performing for the young set. Five hundred people attended.

"I didn't have to lift a finger. I just enjoyed. As the newlyweds left, I helped Kim change her clothes. Alex's parents presented them with a

100

At Kim's wedding in 1972. Connie, Alex, Kim, Alex's parents, Adonna and Raymond Gomez.

brand new car, a surprise added gift. The happy couple left for their Mexican honeymoon. It was a wonderful day for all of us."

Shortly, Connie left for Hawaii, transporting only her music and clothes, leaving other items in storage. She had lost interest in material things. She wanted to clear the decks, create a place for a new beginning, "...so God could fill it completely with His love and beauty."

Now fifty-one years old and alone again, Connie pondered her future.

"Could I make a living again so I may support myself, my children, and my mother? I had some security, for my mother had helped me save during the more auspicious years. How long would that modest savings last? I did not want another divorce. I could not face it. Was I in a state of depression? I was so full of guilt, for I still believed so strongly that 'I was my brother's keeper.'"

101

At church in Honolulu, Connie sought help. She attended Sunday services, and asked for counseling. She met with her pastor and recounted her recent struggles.

"You're struggling with two powers," she explained to Connie," the power of good and the power of evil. In our church we do not accept the idea of sin. Some people express God more perfectly than others."

Connie remained in Hawaii for a few years performing one-night tributes to Tommy Dorsey. She performed with the comedians Allen and Rossi and was criticized in the *Honolulu Star Bulletin*, citing **Miss Haines is as wholesome as Mom's apple pie. Allen and Rossi material is rated triple X.**

Her son Robert joined her in Hawaii, but he was not as happy as she. Racial violence against *Haoles*, as caucasians are called there, get the worst of it in the schools. The Hawaiian people were kind, and mostly full of love, but even in Hawaii racial bitterness existed.

At the Royal Hawaiian Monarch Room, Connie sang all her songs, as well as some Hawaiian tunes like "Little Grass Shack" and "I'll Remember You," written by the late Kui Lee.

Del Courtney visited Connie in Hawaii and once again displayed his jealousies, accusing her of disgusting, outlandish things.

"I just couldn't take that. I burst into tears."

After a four day attempt at reconciliation, Del and Connie both realized it was no use. Del went back to California. The divorce shortly followed.

"I expect to re-marry," he insisted to Connie, "I do not expect to remain alone for the rest of my life."

Moving Forward

RENEWAL AND REWARDS

"Since I essentially was a woman alone, I enrolled in a seminary and studied the Bible, both Old and New Testament. The scriptures have guided me and instilled strength throughout my life, but I hungered to study with the scholars.

"I graduated in 1976, after three years of study and began teaching. Not preaching, mind you. Teaching. When I speak in churches and auditoriums, it's to inspire people towards the love of God, not the fear of him. It's the good news of Jesus Christ. In my humble way I wish to remind others that God is waiting to help everyone. Just 'ask and you shall receive.' God is love and that love dwells in all of us. During my 'graduation period,' my daughter Kim blessed me with a granddaughter, Monica, and my son, Robert, joined the United States Coast Guard at seventeen."

With time on her hands, Connie happily hit the gospel trail once again. Selecting Rex Allen, an established, well-known trombonist, to direct the orchestra, she resumed travel with her partners Jane, Rhonda, and Beryl.

"Funny, the musician on the bass fiddle was Catholic, the guy at the piano was Mormon, the guy on drums was Jewish, and

Robert De Haven, Jr. in the Coast Guard, 1974.

Rex, our trombonist and leader, was Presbyterian. Only God could have arranged things that way. Certainly, I didn't. We were a *bona fide* ecumenical group.

The year Connie Haines faced deadly cancer was 1982. She wasn't given much hope to survive it. She refused, however, to accept that probability. Her lifelong, ongoing incentive to thrive and sing, as always, dominated her personality.

"I had been on a very long Big Band tour when, one night, I felt the presence of a lump under my right arm. I thought it was just another cyst, for I'd had many of those surface during my life and hopefully thought it would disappear like the others."

With a careful eye on the situation she began daily self-examinations only to find the lump growing larger. Ironically, she happened to be performing for several medical conventions, and although inclined to speak to one of the doctor's about it who were present, she felt shy, finally rejecting the idea.

"I felt no panic because I figured cancer would never hit me. So I kept up performing week after week. Then one night—about three a.m.—I awoke with a start, sat straight up and felt the lump. It had increased to about the size of a ping-pong ball. It was as if God had spoken to me saying, 'This is very serious, Connie. Quit the tour and go see a doctor.'"

Connie discontinued the tour and headed for her Los Angeles home.

After the initial surgery, she was informed that she indeed had contracted breast cancer with three tumors in each breast and seven in her lymph glands. The doctors had performed a lumpectomy, hoping for better news.

"Then, with such distressing news under my belt, we had to go all the way—a double mastectomy plus forty-eight lymph glands had to be removed. Afterwards, they placed me on three years of chemotherapy, administered weekly. But, I can honestly say that with my positive attitude and complete faith in God I never lost my hair; I never got sick, and I never missed a show while on the road. I know for sure that I literally sang my way back to better health."

While undergoing chemotherapy, Connie realized she wanted to help others to overcome their cancer, so she founded the Connie Haines Cancer Foundation complete with support groups and counseling services.

"I knew the power of the mind was more powerful than any catastrophic disease. I knew the power of positive attitude would always work for me, as it always had. I knew there was a direct link between attitude and health, and with God's help I would be healed."

Now 1985, Connie moved back to her home in Florida. She needed some settling down.

"One day in 1987, I had just read in the *Tampa Tribune* that my revered friend Bob Hope was coming to Tampa, when I heard the phone, and a voice inquired, 'Is that you, Connie? This is Bob—Bob Hope!' What a great surprise to hear Bob on the line. He invited me to join with

Connie with daughter Kim, 1985.

him in appearances around the Florida area for a few months. 'You bet I will, Bob,' I said."

Connie had first sung with Hope when she was only eighteen, on a radio show called "Command Performance" with Frank Sinatra and Bing Crosby also as guests.

"I remember the show's cute script. All the guys were fighting over who was going to escort me to dinner. You can imagine the fun I had with Bing, Bob, and Frank. Even though it was a written script, they ad-libbed a lot and made it even more fun."

The big affair with Bob Hope was held at the Fountainbleu Hotel for the Hope National Parkinson's Disease Foundation. He had instituted the foundation in 1968.

"It was an elegant affair. The ladies and men were adorned with large gold *Hope* medallions, hanging from blue satin ribbons around their neck. It was a star-studded affair with celebrities Phyllis Diller, Lucille Ball, President Gerald and Betty Ford, Dick Clark, Steve Allen, and others who sat on the Honorary Board."

Comedian Jack Carter was also on the bill. Connie hadn't worked with him for many years. As usual, Bob's wife, Dolores, sang beautifully. Bob was an unbelievable eighty-four years old at the time. It was the occasion of Bob and Dolores' 53rd wedding anniversary. The show always closed with Bob singing his signature theme "Thanks for the Memory" with Dolores on one arm and Connie on the other.

"It was great performing at Disney World with Ray McKinley's Big Band. It was a double treat because many of my friends from Jacksonville traveled there just to watch me perform. Because most of my work had kept me in California most of my life, it was grand to be back in Florida again. My mother was going to celebrate her 90th birthday. She was happy, healthy, and still full of energy."

In late January, Connie flew to New York to appear on Joe Franklin's popular television interview show, where she was able to speak to millions about her newly established Connie Haines Cancer Foundation and Living Center. It became her mission to inspire others to overcome cancer just as she had.

"Don't ever give up! Keep positive in attitude! You can be victorious! This is my message! The moment I walked into my home upon the return from New York—the White House called. Through the American Cancer Society, who had heard of my efforts and brought them to the attention of the President, I had been chosen to receive the Courage Award of 1988. I was overwhelmed." The American Cancer Society also appointed her to be a National Spokesperson during official ceremonies in the White House Rose Garden where she was honored by President Ronald Reagan, who personally handed her the award.

"But, before that, I had to fulfill a twenty- city contract on the east and west coasts of Florida. It's known as the condominium circuit."

After the event at the White House, Connie flew to Boca Raton, Florida to perform with the Pop Symphony, a seventy-five piece orchestra. That marked her first performance of what she called her symphony tours. Then, she was off to Atlantic City to perform an additional four weeks at the Atlantis Hotel Casino with a swinging band of top musicians from New York.

"Then it hit me. Whammo!. Neck surgery. I couldn't sing any more until they repaired the torn, popped muscles in my neck, and at last I had found a marvelous surgeon in New York, Dr. James Smith, who agreed to perform the reconstructive surgery, after many doctors had turned me down for various reasons. What a harrowing experience! I asked myself, 'Would I ever be able to sing again?' Singing wasn't just a livelihood, it was my life. The joy of my life. It is my way of receiving love from others through their applause and attention. It's also a form of security. It's also my way of expressing God. What would I do if I could not sing? Fear and doubt crept in, due to many months of pain, but I persisted and never lost hope or faith. It was difficult. I really had to work overtime with my positive thinking approach to life, but, as before, it always paid off."

Still adorned with neck supports and an occasional brace, Connie was determined to continue performing. By October, with great diligence and effort, she appeared once again on the cruise circuit. The cruises also offered time between for rest.

"Since the surgery I've completed ten concerts, including one in the Grand Ballroom of the Waldorf Astoria in New York. Oh! Yes, I was tired, but happy.

"During the period from January through March of 1989, it transpired again for me. We were back on tour. Me, a grandmother, still on the road like the Dorsey-Sinatra days of the forties and fifties. This time it was with the music of Harry James, under the direction of Fred Radke."

Connie Haines and her troupe traveled through seventy-one cities in three months. Instead of a basic Greyhound, like in the early days, they traveled in a luxurious $200,000 Mercedes-Benz bus appointed with two television sets, videos, telephones, and a complete kitchen. Quite a different story from the early Big Band traveling days. The bus easily covered up to 500 miles a day. Heading towards Florida, the troupe had already covered Southern California, part of Arizona, Texas, Oklahoma, and Louisiana. Florida cities included Tallahassee, Melbourne, Fort Myers, Clearwater, and Sarasota. After that they toured throughout the state of Georgia.

"The highlight of our trip was an evening at Bob Hope's Cultural Center in Palm Springs, California. The theater resembled the magnificent New York Metropolitan Opera House. Jane came down from Santa Barbara, and so did my old friends Elaine and Jack La Lanne. Beryl stopped in between her cruise ship gigs. It was more like a vacation instead of work. In San Diego, we played the huge Sports Arena. Flowers were brought to me onstage after each performance. Here the Big Bands are very much alive. The show was sponsored by a collective group of dance clubs and studios."

In Clearwater, Florida, Connie's appearance drew two thousand people at Ruth Eckerd Hall. She always closes her eyes after performing Ervin Drake's beautiful song "I Believe." When she opened them, everyone was standing and cheering, some bestowing upon her fresh bouquets of roses.

Many have wondered why Connie hasn't retired. She is now beyond her seventy-fifth year.

"Never, never, never! Why quit something that provides me with the happiest, most fulfilling moments of my life? God granted me this gift of a singing voice, and I feel that I must use it. That is to say, there are also sacrifices to talk about here. Most of the singers who have traveled the circuit as I have remain un-married today. Among them are Rosemary Clooney, Kay Starr, Peggy Lee, Anita O'Day besides myself. After an exciting lifetime in front of the public, receiving all the applause and love from that audience, there is no way we could have settled for life with an ordinary married- life partner. That, for us, would declare life to be empty, without depth. In show business, every day is a new beginning. Look at Bob Hope or George Burns. George had signed contracts beyond his 100th year and almost made it. So, sacrifice it is—a lonely life after the applause dies, but I would not trade it for anything else."

Connie with George Burns.

Enjoying a full-blown career, Connie appeared once again at all the great venues, especially at Atlantic City's Atlantis Hotel. It was full circle as she followed Frank Sinatra Jr., as Frank Sinatra Sr. followed her. She was only sixteen when she and Sinatra appeared at the very same place, the Atlantic City Steel Pier, with Harry James' Orchestra. Then, as now, her act was sold out for an entire month. She had re-invented herself again.

During 1990, Connie Haines spearheaded her act towards a new direction. Instead of headlining a Big Band classic show or with "ghost bands" with musicians mostly unknown to her, she decided to produce her own show and hand-pick each musician. She named it Connie Haines Big Band Show, a salute to her former bosses Harry James and Tommy

Dorsey, and featured Charley Raymond on trumpet and Paul O'Connor on trombone. She felt in control of her career and was booked everywhere a plane or train could take her.

"It was a wonderful tour. Warren Covington and the Pied Pipers shared the bill with me often." Warren had acquired ownership of the Pied Pipers in the early seventies and toured for many years until he sold it in 1997 to lead singer Nancy Knorr and retired to Florida with his wife, Sylvia.

While in California, Connie visited her three life-long friends, Jane Russell, Rhonda Fleming, Beryl Davis, their husbands, and old friends Jack and Elaine La Lanne.

At the New Jersey State Fair the troupe once again saluted Harry James, and in Eisenhower Park on Long Island they paid tribute to Tommy Dorsey. The tour moved south to Fort Myers, Florida; they performed at the Barbara Mann Theater, the Van Wezel Hall in Sarasota, and many other theaters on Florida's east coast.

"I never believed in aging or retirement. I always keep moving, keeping that brain active. I advise you to exercise—take long walks, set new, exciting goals, because if you think right, eat right, you will remain healthier. Stay God-centered always and there's nothing you can't accomplish."

In December, 1990, Connie was called to appear on her old singing partner Frank Sinatra's 75th Birthday television special.

"How exciting it was to be on the show. Frank was so pleased; after all, we had been friends for over 60 years. Oh, my God, sixty years! Well, I sang with the Manhattan Transfer vocal group, and, just like the old days, I stared at Frank while I sang to him. His offstage wink told me he remembered.

Ella (Fitzgerald), Tony Bennett, and Peggy Lee were also on the show. So were those wonderful singers Kay Starr, Tony Martin, Helen O'Connell, Helen Forrest, Martha Tilton, Kitty Kallen, and Fran Warren. For all, and especially for me, it was a memorable evening."

In January of 1991, Connie appeared at the opening of Merv Griffin's Resorts Hotel in Atlantic City with all proceeds going to the American Cancer Society. Connie represented the society as its official spokesperson.

In 1993, Connie's itinerary rivaled her early days with James and Dorsey as she took once again to the road:

Connie and her friend Debbie Reynolds, 1998.

Connie with vocalists Martha Tilton and Peggy Lee in 1943.

With "Mr. Television" Milton Berle, 1990.

With old friend Danny Thomas, 1990.

THE CONNIE HAINES ITINERARY
FROM 1993 TO 1999

1993 THROUGH 1996

1993

TAMARAC, FLORIDA in Century Village—Deerfield Beach, she appears in "A Season of Stars" with vocalist Julius La Rosa and entertainers/dancers Donald O'Connor and Joel Grey.

1994

ST. FRANCISVILLE, LOUISIANA: The Connie Haines show in the grand salon aboard the Mississippi Queen on January 28. On the New Year's Eve show Connie appears with Herb Jeffries, Duke Ellington's famous vocalist of "Flamingo" fame. She delivers her legendary rendition of "Will You Still Be Mine," one of her best-loved recordings.

1995

Connie appears with the Ink Spots in "A Salute to Artie Shaw," singing "For Once in My Life" and "Sunny Side of the Street," SEAL BEACH, CALIFORNIA in August of 1995, she appears with bandleader/vocalist Tex Beneke, of "Chatta-nooga Choo Choo" fame at the Amphitheater, both performing the music of his former boss, Glenn Miller.

In KEY LARGO, FLORIDA, Connie appears in Central Park singing her book of swing. At L.A.'s Ambassador's 20th anniversary spectacular, she appeared with Warren Covington's Pied Pipers and Bill Elliot's Swing Orchestra back-to-back with Mel Tormé, Terry Gibbs and Buddy DeFranco's big band in December as a guest with the Sammy Kaye Orchestra on the American Hawaii Cruise on the *SS Constitution*.

1996

Connie appeared in the Academy Plaza Theater in Hollywood with Horace Heidt, Jr. and his band with Tony Martin and Peter Marshall; with her own band for the American Red Cross with Sergio Mendes and Ray McKinley and his orchestra at Epcot Center; with Jane Russell, Beryl Davis, and Rhonda Fleming singing "When the Saint's Come Marching In," to a sold-out crowd at the Belleview Mido Resort Hotel in CLEARWATER, FLORIDA; with singers Margaret Whiting and Kay Starr and the Jimmy Dorsey Orchestra at Barbara Mann Hall in CLEARWATER; In L.A. with the Society of Singers band under the direction of (the other) Ray Charles singing "I Am What I Am."

1998

Reviving the tunes of World War II, Connie saluted the USO with her Stars and Stripes Review, at the Taj Mahal in ATLANTIC CITY, NEW JERSEY in November of 1998. And the list of performances goes on and on sharing stages with Eydie Gormé and Steve Lawrence, and country super-guitarist Chet Atkins, on FLORIDA'S Senior Expo's throughout the Sunshine State right up into 1999.

Connie's premier CD in 1997, a tribute to torch singer Helen Morgan, showcased Connie's clear, non-big band voice, backed by an orchestra of top Los Angeles studio players led by leader/arranger Lew Raymond and featuring solos by jazz guitarist Barney Kessel and trumpeter Frank Beaches. This group of musicians was composed of mostly jazz players.

"We did the songs in one take because we had to do six songs in three hours. We had no time for re-takes. Anyway, the first take is always the best."

She loved delivering the wonderful melodies "Why Was I Born," "Why Do I Love You?" "Bill," "They Didn't Believe Me," and that sweet tune from *Showboat*, "Make Believe."

"I know why I was born; I was born to sing. I just love the song. With this tune you have to hit the highest notes. Doing these kind of songs is nothing new to me. I have played Julie in *Showboat* many times. Performing on albums with these great songs allows me an opportunity to live the song as an actress. And, I can't believe I was recording again after all these years."

Today, Connie's voice is different. Her voice is vibrant with a full two-octave. The Southern mood persists as in all her work. The voice is more delicate—smoother, but can easily project more volume when needed. She adjusts to each setting. On the bandstand with a Big Band she is in her element, but she can also sing with romantic strings, which has always emphasized her versatility as a vocalist.

114

"It was a great joy to record these great songs. I gave them my rhythm twist. I'm a rhythm singer; my *forte* has always been in the blues. Helen Morgan was a wonderful singer. She had a pure voice. When I was with Tommy Dorsey, Frank did all the ballads and I did all the swing numbers. When I sing a ballad, my voice is pure. A lot of the girl band singers couldn't swing. Ella Fitzgerald and I were the original swing singers in the era."

It was producer Dave Pell who selected Connie for the Morgan tribute album, although he was unaware that Connie had played the role of Julie in the Oscar Hammerstein, Jerome Kern musical. "She was sure great to work with. It was very easy to say to her, 'Okay that's great, let's go to the next tune.' And she would say, 'Can't I hear it?' I'd say, 'No, you go on and we'll listen afterwards.'"

Together, old friends and singing partners Jane Russell and Connie embarked upon a Holland-America cruise in 1998. Jane had founded the organization WAIF over thirty years ago and lobbied in Washington to pass a bill favoring international adoption. She is still actively working to this day with hard-to-place children.

"While we were cruising, Jane gave interviews, autograph sessions for her book, and even sang a few songs with me. "

Today, in June 1999, Connie Haines has organized her all- star swing band with trumpeter Bob Switzer, bass player John Lamb, drummer Kenny Loomer, and pianist Hal Vincent to play at the Baypointe Supper Club in Seminole, Florida, close to her Clearwater home. She belts out all her songs featured on albums from the beginning of her career to the present.

"I'm still the kid singing with the band while everyone dances. I had been seeking a supperclub for my singing and finally found it at the Baypointe." Her shows are sold out for weeks in advance. For her the feeling is the same whether it's 1940 or 2000. The audience

Opening night at Florida's Baypointe Supper Club, June 1999.

includes many fans, now retired in Florida, who grew up with the Big Bands and baby boomers who simply love her music. Her singing remains obvious throughout—obvious that her love of singing and performing miraculously goes on and on. Here, she speaks of how she sang her way back from cancer, and she signs her CDs and tapes, with sales to benefit the American Cancer Society. She closes each show with a smashing duet of Cole Porter's "S'Wonderful" with her regular guest vocalist Paulette Pepper. She is at home singing with just about anyone old or young, male or female, Big Band or small band. For her it's the music.

Here we are with a seasoned, legendary performer, Connie Haines, the little girl Big Band singer, who has sang with them all, and remains a valid contender. We have now entered the next Millennium. Connie will be approaching the age of——well, it really doesn't matter, does it, because she will be singing for us like she always has no matter what her age, or ours.

"And, without reservation, I give all the credit to God for my voice and my ability to sing all those wonderful songs that make so many people happy." Sure, rock and roll remains king. Broadway is working revivals; the record business for the bands and their vocalists are diminishing, but new stars are coming along. A young girl named Diana Krall has been singing some of the standards, so will more like her follow? Perhaps. Some of the greats vocalists are gone: Frank Sinatra, Mel Tormé, Dean Martin, Nat "King" Cole, Ella Fitzgerald, Helen Forrest, Guy Mitchell, Bing Crosby, and Joe Williams. Senior citizen Jerry Vale is still performing fifteen to twenty gigs a year. As is Johnny Mathis, Al Martino, Andy Williams, Frankie Laine, and Julius La Rosa. Doris Day, Kitty Kallen, Jo Stafford, Peggy Lee, Perry Como, and Frances Langford are still with us but not performing. Lynn Roberts, Rosemary Clooney, Patti Page, Patty Andrews, and Anita O'Day are still at it from time to time, some more than others.

At this writing, some say it's encouraging that people are once again dancing to big bands. Can we actually allow ourselves to hope this is a true trend and not just a summer romance? It's also true that the big business forces that run the recording business have a great investment in all shades of rock and roll. They also treasure their tremendous profits derived from consumers who have been fed nothing but a solid rock and roll diet with, however, some exceptions. Does that mean there will some day be another Connie Haines or Helen Forrest for us to enjoy? Only time will tell.

Connie Haines, however, is working the hardest as she always has. Her enthusiasm is contagious, especially to those around her. More than any other surviving vocalist of the Big Band Era, Connie Haines has performed the most and at more places. Her story is *the* story.

"Today, I have so many contracts coming up. A special affair for Donald Trump; an eight-day one-nighter tour over ten days time on the other side of Florida, and a pop symphony tour in New Jersey in the year 2000 with an eighty-piece orchestra. I'll never quit-never."

"She tires me out just thinking of what she does every day," Jane Russell said from her California home.

"Since my new supper club engagement is taking up much of my time promoting, making personal appearances, and rehearsing, I am happy to say I'm sold out for many weeks. Isn't it exciting? And, even more exciting is that my granddaughter, Monica Gomez, who is just twenty-four, is persuing a career on Broadway—she dances and sings—and has even appeared in some small parts. I hope she continues a life in music. Maybe some day a book may be written about her career."

In April, 1999, Dr. Kenneth A. Kool of Narberth, Pennsylvania wrote a letter to Ed Kline of radio WPEN in Bala Cynwyd, Pa.:

"Funny thing, Ed. I listen to you all the time and just take it for granted. Woke-up tonight as you made that really wonderful and sensitive presentation of Connie Haines.

"A tiny girl, beautiful, wonderful, and so full of Life! And so very caring of others. She was so giving to others. Still is. One in a few million.

"I'll go on with some other things about her, if you don't mind. Once, a few years ago, I got together with her at the New Jersey State Fair. I mostly watched her rehearse with the band. Don't recall his name, but he was a brilliant trumpeter. Sort of a subdued Harry James style. But, to his credit, he only played with intonations that 'backed' Connie. A great horn that served to accentuate Connie.

"Then, afterwards, endless people, mostly women, came up front, hugged and kissed Connie, and some, with old memories, cried tears of joy. You had to be there to realize how intense the feeling was. They flooded the tent under which she was working for all of us. Connie is an inspirational being. And was so when she sang in a church choir in L.A. in the 1940s. That was in Hollywood where she lived then. Probably the mid to late 40's. She was to have some tough trips later on, like with the Dorsey Band, which had a tough drummer. Her 'mom' was often with her, but not always. Anyway, Connie is a 'survivor.'

"Last thing, Ed. Around 1949-50, Connie and Sarah Vaughan came out of a meeting with Dave Garroway in his office in Chicago.

Arm-in-arm, laughing, hugging, kidding, and oblivious to the world around them. A beautiful moment to see.

"I just felt I had to write you to thank you for your on-going welcome into my house and to say some things about a beautiful person, Connie Haines. Even her best friends could not have done it as well as you did."

End of story!

Connie Haines

with
Ray Block and his Orch.

Walter Winchell
In New York

Connie Haines starts at Baltimore's Club Charles the 16th. Her Signature platter of "You Made Me Love You" is a ding-dong-dilly. Arthur Pollack's play reviews were always fair and made sense... his "demotion" to the editorial dept. will bring enlight... confused...Comden and Green's "Bonjour...

WILL YOU STILL BE MINE

YOU MADE ME LOVE YOU

Sig 15168

Connie Haines is an exclusive Signature artist.

Signature
records

Signature Records, 601 W. 26th St., New York

118

CONNIE HAINES MUSICAL FACTS

RECORDINGS:

WITH HARRY JAMES:
"Comes Love"

"All of Me"

"I Can't Afford to Dream"

"Don't Worry 'bout Me"

WITH TOMMY DORSEY—SOLOS
"What is This Thing Called Love"

"Swing Time up in Harlem"

"Buds Won't Bud"

"I'm Nobody's Baby"

"Will You Still Be Mine"

"And So Do I"

"Sunny Side of the Street"

WITH TOMMY DORSEY, FRANK SINATRA AND THE PIED PIPERS
"Snootie Little Cutie"

"Oh! Look At Me Now"

"Let's Get Away from It All"

"I'll Never Smile Again"

"Friendship"

"I'll Take Tallulah"

"Dolores"

GOLD RECORDS
"You Made Me Love You"

"Ole Man Mose is Dead"

"Will You Still Be Mine"

"For Once in My Life"

"Que Será, Será"

"Mississippi Mud"

"Sunny Side of the Street"

"Why Was I Born?"

"Can't Help Lovin' That Man of Mine"

"Do, Lord"

IN THE 50S, 60S, & 70S.

"You Made Me Love You"

"He Wears a Pair of Silver Wings"

"Ole Man Mose is Dead"

"How It Lies"

"Pink Shampoo"

"Teasin'"

"How Come You Do Me?"

"Dark Town Strutter's Ball"

"Alexander's Ragtime Band"

"La Vie En Rose"

"Little Things Mean a Lot"

"When My Dream Boat Comes In"

"Can't Help Lovin That Man of Mine"

"Why Was I Born?"

"Mississippi Mud"

"Accentuate the Positive"

"Vaya Con Dios"

ALBUMS

"Lover Man" with The Oscar Peterson Trio

"Tribute to Helen Morgan"

"Show Boat"

"Irish Eyes"

"I Am What I Am"

"The Great Tommy Dorsey" with Connie Haines and the Pied
    Pipers

"A Religious Album"

MOTOWN SOUND

THE FIRST WHITE SINGER ON MOTOWN RECORDS, 14 SIDES, WRITTEN BY SMOKEY ROBINSON.

"What's Easy for Two is Hard for One"

"For Once in My Life"

"Walk in Silence"

WITH JANE RUSSELL, RHONDA FLEMING AND BERYL DAVIS

24 HIT GOSPEL RECORDS AND THREE ALBUMS

"Do, Lord"

"The Magic of Believing"

"Make a Joyful Noise"

"Unto the Lord"

"Jacob's Ladder"

MOVIES

Las Vegas Nights with Frank Sinatra, Tommy Dorsey, Robert Preston

A Wave, A War, and A Marine

Moon Over Las Vegas

Duchess of Idaho

Twilight on the Prairie

Salt Water Cowboy

TELEVISION

A two year series with Frankie Laine as Mr. & Miss Rhythm

Texaco Star Theater with Milton Berle

Bob Hope Special with Bing Crosby & Frank Sinatra

Ed Sullivan Show

Eddie Cantor Show

Perry Como Show

Jackie Gleason Show

Red Skelton Show

Jack Benny Show

Abbott & Costello TV Special

Connie's friend from her Motown days, Smokey Robinson.

Frank Sinatra's TV Birthday Show
Ralph Edward's "This is Your Life"

Broadway Musical Tours

West Side Story
Finian's Rainbow
Come Blow Your Horn
Show Boat

Night Club Performances

Atlantis Hotel, Atlantic City
Cocoanut Grove, Hollywood

Copacabana, New York
Waldorf-Astoria, New York
Palmer House, Chicago
Riviera, Sahara, & Tropicana Hotels, Las Vegas
Roosevelt Hotel, New Orleans
Harrah's, Reno
Harrah's Lodge, Lake Tahoe
Taj Mahal, Atlantic City
Disneyworld, Florida
Disneyland, California

WHITE HOUSE PERFORMANCES

FOUR PRESIDENTS:
Dwight D. Eisenhower
John F. Kennedy
Lyndon B. Johnson
Ronald Reagan

December, 1999, Jane Russell visits Connie at Clearwater, Florida. They sing together once more.

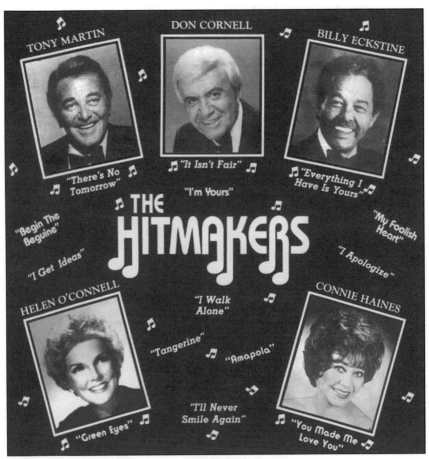

A star among stars, 1997.

CONNIE HAINES

Sings A
Tribute To
Helen Morgan

1. Why Was I Born
   (Previously unreleased version)
2. They Didn't Believe Me
3. Yesterdays
4. Broken Hearted
5. Make Believe
6. Mean To Me
7. Can't Help Lovin' That Man
8. Don't Ever Leave Me
9. More Than You Know
10. The Way You Look Tonight
11. Why Do I Love You
12. Bill
13. Why Was I Born

CONNIE
HAINES

Sings A
Tribute To
Helen Morgan

PRODUCED BY DAVE PELL
Arranged and Conducted
by Lew Raymond

Recording Engineer: Thorne Nogar
Liner Notes, with personal
comments from Connie Haines,
by Eliot Tiegel

Recorded Direct to 2-Track Stereo
at Radio Recorders, Hollywood,
California on July 26 and 30, 1957
Originally released as
TOPS/MAYFAIR STEREO 96065

DIGITAL MASTERING FROM
ORIGINAL SESSION TAPES

℗1997 Pickwick Communications, Inc. ©1997 Sinitar Entertainment, Inc.
Manufactured and distributed in the USA by Sinitar Entertainment, Inc., WARN-
ING: All Rights Reserved. Unauthorized duplication is a violation of applicable
laws. Disc made in USA or Canada. Printed in USA. VISIT US ON THE WORLD-
WIDE WEB AT http://www.simitar.com

0 82551 55472 0

55472

125

ABOUT THE AUTHOR

Richard Grudens of Stony Brook, New York, was initially influenced by Pulitzer Prize dramatist Robert Anderson, New York Herald Tribune columnist Will Cuppy, and mystery writer Dashiell Hammett. In his early years, Grudens worked his way up from a page in NBC studios in New York to newswriter for such names as H.V. Kaltenborn and John Cameron Swayze. He was a feature writer for Long Island P.M. Magazine (1980-86) that led to his first book, *The Best Damn Trumpet Player*.

His other books are *The Song Stars*—about the girl singers (1987), *The Music Men*—about the men singers (1998), and *Jukebox Saturday Night*—More Memories of the Big Band Era (1999), *Jerry Vale, A Singer's Life* (2000) and *Magic Moments*—The Sally Bennett Story (2000).

Commenting about the book *Jukebox Saturday Night* in 1999, Kathryn Crosby said, "Richard Grudens is the musical historian of our time. Without him, the magic would be lost forever. We all owe him a debt that we can never repay."

Bob Hope and Richard Grudens talk about Connie Haines' triumphant career.

Top: Connie's dear mom with a young
Patty Andrews of the Andrews Sisters.
Right: Connie and special friend,
Roseanne Young, 1998.

Connie and Jane today, 2000.

CELEBRITY PROFILES PUBLISHING
BOX 344 Main Street
STONY BROOK, NY 11790

(631) 862-8555 • FAX (631) 862-0139

The BEST DAMN TRUMPET PLAYER   Copies _____
ISBN 1-57579-011-4   196 Pages   55 Photos
Price $15.95

****

The SONG STARS   Copies _____
ISBN 1-57579-045-9   240 Pages   60 Photos
Price $17.95

****

The MUSIC MEN   Copies _____
ISBN 1-57579-097-1   250 Pages   70 Photos
PRICE $17.95

****

JUKEBOX SATURDAY NIGHT   Copies_____
ISBN 1-57579-142-0   250 Pages   70 Photos
PRICE $17.95

****

NAME _____

ADDRESS_____

CITY, TOWN, STATE_____ ZIP CODE_____

Include $ 3.00 for Priority Mail (2 days arrival time) for up to 2 books.

Enclose check or money order. Order will be shipped immediately.

For CREDIT CARDS, please fill out as shown below:

Card #_____ Exp. Date_____

Signature_____

VISA ___AMEX ___ DISCOVER___MASTER CARD___(CHECK ONE)

Coming in Spring 2000

SNOOTIE LITTLE CUTIE — The Connie Haines Story $17.95

JERRY VALE — A Singer's Life $18.95

INDEX

129